THE YEAR I LIVED WITH A PSYCHIC

The Year I Lived With a Psychic

Louise Piper

Sayre Street Books

The Year I Lived With a Psychic

First edition: August 2019

ISBN: 978-1-987849-74-5

This book is not intended as a substitute for the medical advice of physicians. The reader should regularly consult a physician in matters relating to his or her health and particularly with respect to any symptoms that may require diagnosis or medical attention.

Author's Note: I have tried to recreate events, locales, and conversations from my memories of them. In order to maintain their anonymity, in some instances I have changed the names of individuals. I may also have changed some identifying characteristics and details such as physical properties, occupations, and places of residence.

1 3 5 7 9 10 8 6 4 2

Contents

Acknowledgments

I wish to express my love and appreciation to Laura and Andrew for believing in me and supporting my unconventional choices; to Martin for listening to me, for pushing me to my limit, and for sharing champagne and giggles with me; to Howard for always providing a bridge over troubled water and being my faithful rock; to Heidi and Neil for opening their hearts and their home to me; to Dan Conroy for agreeing to join me on my creative journey and making the perfect design for this book; to José Luis for sustenance, intellectual debate, and a magical mystery tour; to Joyce for all the laughter, the tears, and showing me I deserve to be happy; and to Michael for reigniting my creative passion and taking me to Joyce.

I would like to extend my profound gratitude to my doctor for recognising that I needed time and space to learn to live my life in a different way and for taking me to Simone, who reminded me that, first and foremost, I am a free spirit.

Foreword

People change. That's a non-negotiable certainty of each of our lives. We grow old, circumstances shape us, we react, we adapt, we fall, we overcome, and in some instances, we completely overhaul our entire identities and begin anew. In the case of the latter, habits and beliefs that once defined us are recognised as the shackles they often are, and one is reborn. Never have I seen such a radical shift, or 'rebirth', as the one undertaken by Louise Piper.

Rewind ten years, and I am sat in yet another English lesson. This lesson, as are all that are taught by Miss Piper, is planned with such meticulous detail that it is almost military. She has a formula for success, and it works. The students, unruly elsewhere in the school, do one of two things: they listen intently, for they are interested, or they pretend to listen, to avoid confrontation. She talks with great alacrity and rhythm, and transitions seamlessly from one section of the lesson to the next. The students know when they are supposed to engage, and when they are supposed to be quiet, and the lesson concludes as the bell begins to ring, and it rings and rings until the final exams and her students flourish once more.

She was a teacher above all others, yet looking back, there was a palpable anxiety about her work. Failures hit her harder than they did anyone else, and her response would always be to work harder, and plan more. Through the fastidiously planned lessons, I still remember Miss Piper's eyes light up when she talked about poetry and, away from the whiteboard, she spoke wistfully about writing a book. I will always know Louise as the greatest teacher I have ever had. A potent combination of dedication and genuine care for her students made her successful, but in those moments that she talked about what could be, it was clear to me that her path would take her away from the classroom.

Even so, imagine my surprise when she told me that she was going to quit her job and move to Spain to live with a psychic so she could write a book. To some, it may have seemed reckless and dangerous, but when I talked to her, and she explained the uncanny series of events that were leading her there, it made more sense to me than anything else in the world.

This book will teach you, as it did me, that no matter how invested in something you are, it's always okay to walk away, even if it's from your entire identity. It's okay to trust your own judgement. It's okay to listen to your soul, and when you do, you might just find the answers you've been looking for in all the wrong places . . .

Jack Saunders

July 2019

THE YEAR I LIVED WITH A PSYCHIC

Prologue

To live is the rarest thing in the world.
Most people exist, that is all.

Oscar Wilde

I perched tentatively on the edge of the enormous reclining chair. Attempting to ease my way into the seat so that my back would be supported, I realized that this left my feet dangling over the edge like a toddler. I extended the footrest so that I wouldn't get pins and needles while I watched the film. To any observer, I must have appeared to be very relaxed.

It was a dark and icy January evening and I had decided to go to the cinema. Surely it would have been more comforting to stream a film at home? But that, I guess, was the problem. Home just didn't feel that comfortable anymore

… if it ever had. Truth be told, I was anything but comfortable in my own skin and found that I was constantly driving here and walking there so that I was never still long enough to feel the swirling agitation within that constantly threatened to explode.

I had been looking forward to the film, *La La Land*, and was completely engrossed by it. My decision to come here had been a good one. However, as the film made its way towards its resolution, I saw the narrative that I had anticipated begin to unravel before me. Usually, that would have impressed me. This time it devastated me. Tears streamed silently down my face. Wow, a powerful film, I thought, rooted in my chair. I vaguely became aware of people in the theatre chatting and moving about before the lights came on. While I hung on to every word of the credits, some were even smiling and laughing. Wait, hold on! I silently admonished them, Don't you think that's the saddest ending you've ever seen? They all seemed blissfully unaware of the tragedy that had unfolded in front of them.

Five days later I sat in my doctor's surgery. I was weeping so much I was barely coherent. He asked how long I had been like this and I explained that I had not stopped crying since Saturday evening after my visit to the cinema. Literally. As I lay in bed falling asleep, the tears would still be flowing, I woke up crying, and cried all day. He asked if there had been a particular trigger? Yes, I replied, I went to watch a film and the ending made me cry. I thought he would laugh at me, but instead he said, "This is more than some work-related stress. I think it's time you went to see somebody."

Introduction

Picture this: you're a well respected teacher of English who has spent a chunk of her life raising two children by herself. And then you reach a scary precipice: your children are now independent adults, your nest is empty, and the career which used to drive you has recently run you over. You've been incredibly successful, but at a cost. Years of working seventy-plus hours a week has left you mentally exhausted. You're a bit lost, wondering who you are and what you really want out of life, and trying to get yourself back on track, when you're randomly asked if you would agree to have lunch with a psychic who wanted to meet you. Here's what happened when I dared to say yes.

For twelve months of my life, I operated as a lens on the life of a psychic. From snapshots to full-blown close-ups, I watched a medium go about her extraordinary, everyday life. From the personal to the professional, my experiences living with the medium, Joyce Vernon, changed my life.

Charlatan. Cheat. Quack. Joyce is aware that many people consider mediums to be con artists who read body language and facial expressions, telling people what they want to hear to trick them out of money. I had not really considered the impact of this judgement from a medium's perspective. Living with Joyce showed me how vulnerable she is to people's harsh opinions and that her gifts also present her with challenges in her day-to-day life. In particular, living with Joyce helped me: to appreciate the importance of listening to our emotions; to realise the need to make brave decisions in order to grow; to be able to distinguish between living a life and merely existing.

Joyce believes we all have spiritual guides and the spirits of passed loved ones who help us in our life. The spirits that help us may change over time according to the needs we have in our lives. Since she is a medium, Joyce is able to channel messages from these spirits. She prides herself on her accuracy and she trusts 100% in Spirit, the collective term for these spirits, and the messages they bring. Her view is that if only we would listen to these messages, we could all save ourselves a lot of pain and heartache from following the wrong pathway. This may seem idealistic and, before I lived with Joyce, I would not have believed it is possible to connect to Spirit in this way.

While researching and writing this book and living with Joyce, we have shed tears of sadness and laughter. At times, this book will share gut-wrenching stories about love and loss. And I will show you the truth of what the life of a medium is really like. There have been spine-tingling moments of awe combined with episodes of frustration. Above all though, I want to show you how the human spirit has the strength and capacity to grow.

1

Coincidences

There are more things in heaven and earth, Horatio,
Than are dreamt of in your philosophy.

Shakespeare, *Hamlet*

I'd never really given much thought to the idea of coincidences and just assumed that they were an inevitable part of life. Other than a *Well* or an *Ooh* to register the recognition, I really didn't think too deeply about whether they had any significance. I now understand that coincidences are not as random as you may think.

The series of coincidences I experienced leading up to meeting Joyce in September 2017 are best described as slow burners. Before I could meet Joyce, it was necessary for me to reconnect with Michael, a school friend of one of my brothers. I had not seen him since he was a teenager, but, three decades later, I found myself bumping into him when I was out and about. We were living in different towns yet somehow our paths would cross and we would catch up briefly on how things were going in our lives.

On a bitterly cold January day in 2017, I ran into him again for a fourth time, but this time in my hometown. As usual, it was Michael who spotted me first and called my name while I was huddled, bracing myself against the elements, looking at my feet. This time, he offered me his number and I hesitated for a moment, not sure where this would lead. I wasn't sure if I was imagining it, but his eyes held my gaze for just a few seconds too long and I wondered if the beginnings of a potential romance were stirring. I was still emotionally fragile and on my guard, but a voice in my head said *What have you got to lose?* Something was urging me to see where it would go. Putting his number in my contacts began a series of events that would lead to me walking away from my career, selling my house, and living in another country.

Michael and I had been seeing each other, sporadically, for a few months when he first mentioned Joyce. At the time, I was still reeling from my burnout, struggling with anxiety and mental exhaustion, and I felt that I needed to get away from it all. Michael suggested that I visit his friend, Joyce, who lives in Spain. However, she was a stranger to me and I felt I wouldn't relax so I decided instead to go and stay with friends in Canada.

It was five months later, a few months after my return from Canada, that Michael mentioned Joyce to me again. She was in the UK visiting her sons and catching up with a case she had been working on with the police. Michael told me that he had been to see her for a reading. His mother, who had been a long-standing client of Joyce's, had recently died and Michael wanted to see if Joyce could connect with her spirit. Joyce was house-sitting at the home of Sarah, one of her close friends who features later in this book, and invited us both for lunch. Joyce would regularly stay at Sarah's home when she visited the UK. I'd always thought that dabbling in spiritual matters might invite discord into my life. But as she said she wanted to discuss a book idea with me, my interest was sufficiently piqued and I agreed.

Arriving at the house, my anxiety was further intensified when I heard the barking of more than one dog from the inside. Since I had been knocked to the ground by a dog as a little girl, I had always been very wary of them. As we stood waiting for Joyce to answer the front-door knock, Michael tried to reassure me: "Don't worry, the large one's quite placid really, it's the small one you have to watch. But he's usually okay with women." *Great*. I felt my body stiffen and my smile began to resemble a grimace.

Joyce immediately sensed my unease, ushered the dogs into the garden, and gave me a long and warm hug. I began to relax, but I was on high-alert. Was the hug simply a ploy so she could read me? I determined to keep my counsel as much as possible and to try not to reveal any thoughts and feelings through my facial expressions.

Michael went to buy some salad to go with the lunch and I was left alone with Joyce. "Ask me anything you want," she enthused. My mind was racing. Should I ask the one question that was bothering me or would that be too confrontational? If I didn't ask the question, would she know I had been too cowardly? Spit it out, I chastized myself.

"Ok, so was that long hug your way of reading me?"

"No, I gave you the hug to help you to relax. You were so uptight about the dogs," she said, taking me by the hand and leading me to the patio doors looking out onto the garden where we watched the dogs happily resting in the sun. Continuing to hold my hand tightly, she reassured me that the dogs posed no threat and that I should relax. Joyce was so warm and comforting, I felt myself let go of the tension. She continued, "No, I don't need to touch a client to give a reading, but it does help me if they are calm and relaxed."

I was nervous about meeting this stranger from a world I didn't understand, but I was also fascinated to hear her talk about her life. And the fact that I was somewhat skeptical? She loved it! I had never met her before, but it was at this first meeting that she asked me if I would write her story for her. She knew from Michael that I was a teacher of English and told me that 'upstairs' had been nagging her for ages to get her book written. Joyce was convinced that Spirit had brought me to her for this reason. At first I thought this was incredulous. However, as I listened to her talking about the damaging nature of fear and the restorative and transformative power of nature, just like the Romantic poets I had read, studied, and taught for many years, I realized I was intrigued by this woman. I sensed I could learn a lot from Joyce and began to wonder if I really could write her book.

I sat at the kitchen table while she busied herself preparing the lunch. Joyce spoke rapidly and ranged through decades of her life sharing random snippets with me, interspersed with a minor evaluation of my current situation: "You've taken steps to improve your happiness, but you're still in the slow lane." She was right. I had only recently resigned my full-time teaching post and felt like a rudderless ship. I had become disaffected with the politics of teaching and knew I wasn't happy, but I didn't know what I wanted to do next. I had moved away from teaching and was now tutoring. This gave me a greater sense of freedom although it was not really a very radical change. As she chatted away, telling me more about her life, she suddenly went to her bag and pulled out a soft toy which she placed in front of me on the kitchen table.

"This is my pet dragon – he won't hurt you. He's called Forrest."

I began to feel some disquiet. To begin with, how many adults do you know that carry a toy—and a dragon, at that—on their person? *Exactly*. How many adults who may do this would so readily set the toy down in front of a complete stranger? But this was not the true source of the disquiet I was feeling. The filing system of my brain quickly located the cause of my unease. Just the day before I had been teaching conversational English to a lovely Polish lady who had recently moved to England with her husband and children. At the end of the lesson, we had a chat to help her to practice:

"Is your daughter happy?" I prompted.

"Yes, she has a pet dog."

"What is the dog's name?"

"Dog is called Forrest."

What an unusual name for a dog, I had thought … *It was an even more unusual name for a toy dragon placed in front of me less than twenty-four hours later.* My eyes widened as I made the connection so I looked down and sipped my tea not wanting Joyce to recognize my unease.

Joyce picked up the conversation: "Forrest is short for Forrest Gump," she explained as she seasoned the chicken before putting it in the oven. I turned away, barely disguising my incredulity. Forrest Gump was my friend's nickname for me since I regularly dragged her along with me on my long walks. Coincidence. Surely, I was just reading too much into everything.

Joyce began to tell me that she had had a long-distance relationship with a partner who lived in Canada. I remembered that I was wearing my maple leaf pendant around my neck and my hand was drawn to conceal it. Just as quickly, I took my hand away again as I thought to myself that there was little point in trying to hide my connection to Canada now. If I didn't start to say something soon, Joyce would imagine me to be a mute!

"Oh, I have a Canadian birth certificate!" I shared with her.

"Really? What part of Canada are you from?" Joyce asked with genuine surprise.

"Ontario," I replied vaguely.

"That's where my friend lives," continued Joyce. Mmm, well a lot of Canadians live in that province, I thought.

"What part of Ontario?" I asked.

"Guelph." There was a silence as I absorbed her response which seemed unbelievable to me.

"That's where I was born," I eventually responded.

"No! Really? Now that has to be a sign. I think Spirit is definitely trying to show us we are meant to work together," Joyce gushed.

Michael returned and over lunch Joyce quizzed us about how we knew each other. She asked if we could remember where we had first bumped into each other. The only place that we could both strongly remember was the time we had come across each other outside of a Waterstones book shop. Instantly, Joyce saw this as another sign that Spirit had brought me to her via Michael to write her book.

Joyce explained that she had started to write her book several years previously; however, she had then become too busy to continue with it. I was seriously thinking about taking on the project of writing her book and wanted to know what had been done so far. I asked her if she still had the draft she had worked on, thinking this would be a useful starting point for me. Joyce explained that she no longer had the laptop she had used and hadn't backed up the draft in any way. Then she remembered that she had sent it as an email attachment so a friend could read it and give her some feedback. I suggested that she look through her "Sent" box to see if she could find it. Joyce pushed the dirty lunch plates to one side and began to look through her emails. This was a laborious task, but eventually she found the email which had been sent to her friend in September four years previously. And who was the friend? Michael who was sat at the table with us! Another coincidence.

Before I left, Joyce invited me to spend a week with her in Spain. This after having spent only a few hours with her. Yet I had never felt so compelled to do something. Something was urging me to be brave and seize the day. It was as if my soul knew I needed to see some fresh horizons.

It perhaps wasn't the smartest move to prepare for my visit by reading a work of fiction, *Beyond Black* by Hilary

Mantel. A well-respected and prize-winning author, she was bound to have done her research. What a treat and a terror! So well written, but so bleak. The protagonist, Alison, is a medium who can never really embrace the land of the living since the dead won't leave her alone. The spirits Alison communicates with were society's dead-beats. And now that they're dead, they have even less to lose. Her new assistant, Collette, struggles to record Alison's story, constantly battling Alison's chaos and resistance from the spirit world. Oh my days, what rock was I lifting?

So, that's how I came to meet Joyce and to begin writing this book. At the time I accepted Michael's number, I could never have predicted that I would begin a journey where I would risk my financial security and even the roof over my head. But that's exactly what I did. And what have I gained? I hope the remaining chapters of this book will show you.

2

Angel Wings

With freedom, books, flowers and the moon,
who could not be happy?

Oscar Wilde

My friends thought I was crazy when I told them I was going to stay with a psychic in Spain, having only met her for lunch the one time. Yet I just felt so sure it would be okay. Landing in Almeria, just four weeks after first meeting Joyce, I admit to panicking – what if it was all a hoax and I'd turned up in a foreign country not knowing the lingo and not having booked a place to stay? Nervously, I sent Joyce a message to say I'd made it to the airport and I would be getting the shuttle bus to Mojácar. Climbing in the bus, I felt like an alien. My pale skin made me look so out of place and I wasn't sure I'd be able to acclimatize to the warm, dry air, having lived in the damp, grayness of England for so long.

The bus dropped me off on the coastal road in the center of Mojácar an hour later. It was a Sunday and early-morning low cloud was clearing to reveal the sky and sea merging on the horizon with a hazy smudge of indigo separating the two. The traffic on the road was scant and a solitary male figure ambled away from me along the pavement to my left. In the stillness, I was easily able to tune into the sound of the sea. Squinting in the bright light, I put on my sunglasses and relaxed into the warmth of the day as I waited for Joyce to come and meet me. I had been in Mojácar for only a few minutes and I was already more attuned to my senses.

Joyce wore large, dark-tinted glasses which made her appearance glamorous and mysterious. Her outfit seemed to be carefully co-ordinated although I now realize that her flair for style means she is able effortlessly to assemble any outfit in seconds. On this day, she wore crisp, white trousers with a flowing, sheer black top. Her long blonde hair was fastened up casually. "Hello! Welcome to Spain.

We're going to have such fun!" she enthused, giving me another one of her warm, welcoming hugs. "Follow me."

Eating lunch together a couple of hours later, the conversation was easy and light. At this stage, it was only her eyes that suggested there was something extraordinary about this woman. Most striking were her pupils against the softness of each iris which alternated between the palest blue and a luminous green. I wondered whether our nearness to the sea, as we sat *al fresco*, was being reflected in her eyes, but since then I have often noticed that her eyes do indeed seem to change color, sometimes even as you are engaged in conversation. Her large eyes are always heavily made up with sweeps of dark eyeliner and metallic brown-green shadows. Black mascara curls her long lashes away from her eyes and her slightly upturned nose is both elegant and appealing. Joyce is a very attractive woman.

On that first day, Joyce seemed perfectly "normal." She sensed my trepidation so there was no mention of the spirit world, only of how she had built a life in Spain. As we lunched, she reeled off the names of all the friends she would introduce me to throughout the coming week.

Waiting for the bus to take us back to her place, one of her friends drove past and quickly stopped to offer us a lift. I came to realize that every person we met that spoke to Joyce had a deep connection with her. They always wanted to pick up on a topic of conversation from thc time before, to recount how a reading she had done for a friend had come to fruition, to share how much better a friend felt since Joyce had offered solace or healing, or to arrange another time to meet for a drink and a catch-up.

At only five feet tall, Joyce is quite short and it is her human, vulnerable self that she calls "little Joyce." This part of her is exactly like the rest of us. Then there is "big Joyce" and this is the whole of her that also incorporates what she refers to light-heartedly as her "spooky" part which enables her to communicate with Spirit. She had first come to live in Spain a couple of years previously. Mojácar is a place that captures the imagination of artists and those wanting to escape the pressures of their work-dominated lives. Since the small village was rejuvenated in the 1960s, something of the "hippie" influence has lingered and there are many people in Mojácar and the surrounding areas that are very open spiritually. A perfect place for Joyce.

I had a lot of questions for Joyce. Just what did it mean that she was a medium? How was her world different from other people's? As we chatted on that first day in Spain, she struck me as warm and intelligent. Not cuckoo, certainly not false. Honestly, more grounded than I was expecting. There were no outward signs, initially, that she was different from the rest of us.

Over the course of the next several days, I saw how her warm and vivacious personality connects to many people. And I was to hear for the first time her now-familiar chortle as she engages in friendly banter with the many people who seem drawn to her like a magnet. Her angel-wing earrings danced and glinted in the sun while she revealed that she did not become a professional medium until much later in her life – in fact not until two marriages and a career in retail management and buying were behind her. Divorced with grown-up sons, she first worked professionally as a medium at a prestigious hotel in the UK.

So how did she end up in Mojácar? She explained that her friend Sam, who has lived there for years, suggested she come to visit. This began a pattern of Joyce visiting Sam a few times a year. She began giving readings to people at various venues in town and her reputation as a medium began to grow. Before long, people were queuing up to receive a reading from her.

Eventually, Joyce decided to be bold and work full-time in Spain. "They will always reward you for being brave," she whispers. She is referring to Spirit. She remembers feeling absolutely petrified as she left behind the close knit community in the UK that had been her home for as long as she could remember and where she had raised her family. Joyce, despite her psychic ability, feels the same insecurities as the rest of us as we go through our lives.

That October night, I settled myself down into Joyce's bed that she insisted I use for the week. There were two beds in the one bedroom, but Joyce decided to give me some space and she slept next door on the sofa in the lounge. My surroundings were so unfamiliar. In front of me an undressed window looked out on to a huge palm tree. The silhouette of its leaves looked like an outstretched hand in my fertile imagination. I would wake from time to time in the night and imagine the hand was reaching in to clutch me. Even more alarming, however, was the carved, wooden angel that hung suspended in the recess of another wooden window frame on my right that looked directly out on to the terrace and the Mediterranean Sea which perpetually hushed a lullaby in the distance. The angel moved constantly and seemed to be agitated by more than the gentle breeze. Whenever I turned to face the window, as I struggled to find sleep, my gaze would meet her knowing eyes and this troubled me.

In the morning, the bobbing angel greeted me serenely and I sensed she had been my sentinel through the night. No longer wary, I now felt comforted by its presence. The creaking of the leather sofa in the next room told me that Joyce was awake and before long we were sitting on her sunny terrace, chatting about her life story, pausing for me to make notes from time to time. Joyce was keen that the book would let people know that our loved ones continue to be with us in Spirit. I learned during this session that she prefers her readings to be done in an intimate one-to-one context and she estimates that she achieves 90% accuracy in these.

Why not 100% accurate? Spirits are so enthusiastic to share messages with Joyce that when she connects to Spirit, she may have a spirit conveying a message for another person she might be seeing in a few days' time. If somebody says this message doesn't make any sense, Joyce lets it go. Eventually it will make sense for whom the message was meant, but at the time of the reading there may be occasional messages that don't seem to fit.

She likes to contain the environment and the process of the reading so that the client is absolutely clear about what information has come through Joyce. It is for this reason that Joyce minimizes dialogue and, typically, she closes her eyes during a reading so she can't see facial responses to the things she is saying. It is important that people leave Joyce knowing that they have not given her any of this information.

It is true that for most of the time when Joyce is doing a reading she will encounter somebody who is open to what she is about to say. You could argue that they are more than open, that they are susceptible to believing what she has to say: they may be vulnerable and are looking for some kind of reassurance. Joyce is always mindful of this and she does not want a vulnerable person to leave her feeling worse. Her conviction is, "If I can't do you any good, I won't do you any harm." Not dissimilar to the way a doctor signs the Hippocratic Oath, she has made this her own personal pledge for the way she will interact with the people who come to see her.

I would witness Joyce take a sharp intake of breath as she began to communicate with Spirit. This became a well-known signal to me that Joyce was about to channel a spirit. During the first week I visited Joyce and observed her giving readings, I felt like a neutral observer. My responsibility was to record what I noticed in my journal. It was the person she was giving the reading to that became wide-eyed, peering toward Joyce intently so that they didn't miss out on any detail. Those who were regular clients would be armed with pen and notebook and would log readings to monitor progress to report back to Joyce at their next meeting. I was trying desperately to rationalize what was going on … it was Joyce who provided all of the information so where was it coming from? Inside of Joyce? Outside of Joyce? I was sat very close to Joyce, but I didn't feel any different physically. Interestingly, I didn't feel scared. Rather, I was excited by this dimension in our lives I had so easily dismissed before.

After Joyce's reading, a couple of days through the week of my first visit to her, we were again sitting on her terrace enjoying the view of the sea and discussing the content for this book. A restless night spent supporting a distressed client via social media and a busy morning channelling Spirit had left Joyce feeling tired. The peaceful surroundings and heat from the sun were soothing to her. Breaking off our conversation, Joyce suddenly asked me, "Is there a Catherine in your family?" I replied no, but that I had a very close friend with that name. A few days before my departure to Mojácar, my friend had come to see me to discuss a family problem that was causing her some agitation. Joyce revealed that the spirits of the paternal grandparents of this friend had now come through to her. This had happened completely out of the blue and I learned that Joyce doesn't need to be in the process of giving a reading for Spirit to communicate with her. Oh my goodness, I thought, there are spirits sharing space with me on the terrace … although I couldn't see or feel anything different.

There was a pause and Joyce inhaled quite sharply. In a very forthright way, Joyce outlined the nature of my friend's problem very specifically and explained that the spirits of her paternal grandparents had some advice for her. She asked me to let Catherine know that she had followed her heart for long enough and it was now time to use her head and to protect herself from more emotional hurt. The message was brief and direct and had been delivered very quickly. I would soon get used to scribbling down spiritual guidance channelled through 'big Joyce' in one of my companion notebooks. My hand quivered as I recorded the information: Joyce had talked about the precise problem my friend had told me about. She knew exactly what my friend's misgivings were and Joyce had relayed the dilemma to me just as my friend had described it to me. I had not mentioned this situation or my friend to Joyce. How could this be?

My friend gladly received this advice from me on my return. She knew the counsel was sound, but there was one thing that surprised her—that it was her paternal rather than maternal grandparents who came through to Joyce. Catherine explained that she had not really known her paternal grandparents as they had died when she was very small. Joyce says that this is not uncommon and that family members who did not have the opportunity to guide you while they were living are often the ones who will guide you spiritually.

As the heat of the third day cooled, the early evening temperature was idyllic for my first introduction to Joyce's landlord, and now friend, José Luis. Joyce gave me the background of how they had met at a party hosted by Pia, the woman who translates at Spanish readings for her. José Luis has known Pia for many years and had heard of "the medium" before he met her at the party. "So, you're the famous Joyce." Always forthright, José Luis had immediately challenged Joyce, "What makes you think you're any good at what you do?"

"Wasn't that a bit intimidating?" I asked.

"It's fine … I understand people's skepticism, I've been there myself," Joyce smiled at me, curling her legs underneath her.

Something must have impressed or intrigued José Luis since he invited her to come to his house to do a reading for him. It was as they were chatting after the reading that Joyce mentioned she was looking for a place of her own. And so Joyce came to live in an apartment situated on the grounds of José Luis' home. It was here that I was to interview the people who feature in this book. And it was here that I came to meet José Luis myself.

As we were sitting on the terrace, the full moon began to emerge in the dimming light. A bottle of *vino blanco* fizzed into tall glasses. "Cheers … so, Louise, tell me, how are you going to do this? This is quite a task, to tell her story. This is a serious business. You must do it justice." I realized at once that José Luis would be a formidable critic since his command of English was exceptional and I understood that José Luis meant that it was my duty to challenge the things I was told.

The following day, I encountered Joyce's spiritual development group. In preparation, I asked Joyce what this involved and she replied with a mischievous grin, "You'll see." During the week I was to shadow Joyce's activities and so I was invited to sit around the table in the African hut, situated on José Luis' side of the garden terrace, with the small group. Four lovely ladies turned up and Joyce made us all tea. I wasn't quite sure what to expect, but I sat with my notebook open and pen poised so that I could record any bits of information I might find useful. So transfixed was I by the events that took place, however, that I had little opportunity to put pen to paper.

To begin with there was warm chatter amongst the women who clearly all knew each other well. The group, consisting of Sarah, Sue, Maxine, Chris and Vickie, had been running for almost twelve months. Maxine had been absent in previous weeks and so there was much to catch-up on the events that had unfolded in her world; Chris was just about to make an exciting four-month tour of India and Bhutan and many enquiries were made about her preparations for this; Vickie was away in England and the women discussed when she was expected to return.

Teas sipped and news gleaned, Joyce announced it was time to begin. The teacher in me recognized Joyce's technique when she said, "Okay, I'm going to start with the person who always sits there worrying that I'm going to pick her next, so if she goes first it will be out of the way." Turning to Chris, who sat next to her, Joyce asked her to make a start. There were some giggles of relief and sympathy from them all, but I sat silently and wondered what she was expected to get "out of the way."

A hush descended within the hut and all eyes looked at Chris, whose eyes were closed. Joyce began to coax Chris to share her communication from Spirit … oh my goodness, I thought to myself, I'm sitting at a table with a group of trainee mediums! I watched as Joyce coached the women who each had a turn at channelling Spirit with messages for somebody at the table. Joyce directed them to ask questions in order to clarify who they were talking to and what the message entailed.

For all of the novices, a common problem was that they became overwhelmed by the emotion of the spirit. Joyce explained that to be an effective medium, you must always be able to distinguish between your own feelings (emotional and physical) and those of the spirit you are connecting with. This helps you to communicate more accurately. In addition, if you start to feel the emotion of the spirit as your own, you are not going to be able to give an effective reading.

Just as I began to feel a tightening in my throat, Joyce explained to the group that if a male spirit tries to communicate through a female medium, this constricted feeling may happen because male vocal cords are thicker than a woman's. It is a very quick sign to show you whether it is a male or female spirit that is communicating with you. I was excited yet somewhat fearful that I seemed to be sharing some of the experiences of the other members of the group. Joyce asked me if I had felt any unusual sensations and told her that there had been a strange sensation in my throat and a feeling that I had sucked on a sherbet lemon. She confirmed that there was a male spirit at my shoulder. I shuddered in response and didn't dare look behind me for the duration of the meeting.

Joyce explained to me that because I was present at the table, Spirit would have assumed that I was open to this learning. They would know I was writing the book and wanted to give me first-hand experience to assist me. Joyce's guides would let Spirit know that the group was open to receiving messages to help them learn and my guides would have permitted the attempt to channel a message through me as I was keen to learn about mediumship to help me write the book. Joyce had already described to me how each one of us has a team of spirit guides who help us in our life. These will change over time as our life circumstances change and they will be in addition to the spirits of passed loved ones who may try to help you from time to time. Remember, though, that before you attempt to connect with anyone other than your personal spirits, that is, your guides or the spirits of loved ones, Joyce recommends that you should learn more from a professional and reputable medium.

Nothing could have prepared me for this first visit to her in Spain. I had some of the most amazing experiences of my life that week, from the fantastic location, waking up to see the sun rise over the Mediterranean, observing Joyce giving people readings and witnessing Joyce channelling Spirit. I left Spain and Joyce utterly committed to the book project. I also left noticing a difference in myself. I had found a purpose and I had taken a risk. Being brave and becoming more in touch with my senses had invigorated me.

3

The Mountains

Beyond the sun, beyond the ether,
Beyond the limits of the starry spheres,
My Spirit, you move with agility.

Charles Baudelaire

When Joyce had first given her landlord, José Luis a reading, the spirits of his parents came through to her. It was evident to Joyce that José Luis' relationship with his mother was a source of unhappiness to him. During my second trip to Mojácar to work with Joyce, this source of José Luis' angst was to rise to the surface. This provided an opportunity for his pain to be healed by Joyce.

On the November evening of my return a month later, the three of us had dinner at a local restaurant. We were discussing José Luis' difficulty sleeping. Every night he seemed to review all of his issues and angst. Sleeping pills were no help. Like many of us, José Luis just wanted some peace, to be able to turn off the internal arguments in his head. Joyce explained that Spirit connects to us when our brain is relaxed. When we are in the process of waking, our brain is in an ideal relaxed state and so this is a time when it is easier for Spirit to connect with us. José Luis' fretful nights meant he rarely experienced that delightful transition between sleep and being fully awake and Joyce believes that, consequently, he missed chances for his loved ones in spirit to communicate with him.

When we are going about our day-to-day activites, one of our deceased relatives may just pop into our minds; Joyce feels that is Spirit connecting with us. Perhaps José Luis' continued unrest was occurring since his sixth sense, or the voice of his soul, felt that it was being suppressed and was continually being argued against by the rational part of his brain. To compound matters, his long, restless nights meant that as dawn was breaking, at just the point he should be waking from a restful sleep, and being open to Spirit or his sixth sense, José Luis would fall into a deep, if short-lived sleep, leaving him in a stupor for the day until the cycle would be repeated the following night.

It was as we were discussing these issues that Joyce connected to the spirit of José Luis' mother, Angelina. She had died over forty years ago, when José Luis, her youngest child, was in his early twenties. At that time, José Luis was working and living in England and had been called back to Spain as his mother lay dying. He spent some time with his desperately ill mother then decided to return to England, feeling that he couldn't bear to watch her die. Part of José Luis' angst relates to the fact he has no recollection of the first six years of his life yet feels there is something troubling about this period. As the youngest sibling of the family, he feels there is no-one left to help corroborate any of his hazy memories or to furnish him with any details of his early life.

As I watched him share his feelings with Joyce, I detected both his frustration at the missing gaps of his early life, and his sadness at the loss of connection with his mother which he felt happened much earlier than when she actually died. The youngest of seven, José Luis feels he was raised by his older sisters even though his mother was present in their lives and I began to appreciate that this man had long felt abandoned by his mother. Joyce told José Luis that the spirit of his mother was sitting on the chair beside him at the restaurant. Joyce became weepy as she felt the emotion of Spirit and let José Luis know that he was born at 5am; he was very strong when he was born, crying straight away. His infant eyes were screwed up as if he did not want to face the shock of being born. Joyce told us that his mother is so proud that he is able to speak English so fluently to us both.

José Luis confided that in her lifetime his mother would have avoided a medium such as Joyce as a result of her social and cultural conditioning; she was a woman whose religiousness came from convention rather than conviction; now, however, José Luis recognizes the irony that his mother's spirit needs Joyce so that she can communicate with her youngest son. Before the end of the reading, the spirit of Angelina asked Joyce to give José Luis the jasper ring that Joyce was wearing; the spirit of Angelina knew that this stone had come from a sacred river in India so thought that this may give her son some spiritual solace. The spirit of Angelina did not want José Luis to wear it necessarily, but she wanted to know that he possessed it. As I watched on, it seemed to me that the spirit of Angelina was making a loving gesture to her son from beyond the grave, symbolically trying to give him some peace. Joyce happily handed over the ring. In Joyce's world jewelry doesn't have material value – rather the value is sentimental. Also, certain metals and stones possess healing or spiritual properties. This was not the first ring she would hand away during my visit, nor would it be the last time she was to be connected to the spirit of Angelina.

On the second day of this second visit to Spain, José Luis had arranged to take Joyce and myself on a trip to a mystery destination. I was intrigued and Joyce was excited. José Luis knew that I had come to do more research for the book and to do some writing. Without knowing where we were going, I was not sure how much research and writing I would manage; however, José Luis seemed utterly invested in the project of the book and so I trusted that his trip would enhance the venture in some way. I was not mistaken.

The first part of the journey took the main coastal road from the arid province of Almeria, westward towards the province of Granada. José Luis drove while Joyce and I enjoyed the changing Spanish vista, our constant companion the mesmerizingly still and glassy Mediterranean, always to the left of our car. Eventually, we turned away from the sea and headed north toward the mountainous terrain of Granada. As we neared the end of our journey, we began our ascent of Las Alpujarras, a region of mountain villages situated on the south side of the Sierra Nevada range. Impressive mountain peaks reached for the infinite bright blue sky. Squat and ugly buildings covered with scrawling graffiti interrupted the ancient panorama from time to time, but only served to intensify our appreciation of the natural and majestic landscape.

Passing a road-side snow symbol, I began to appreciate just how high we were. Instinctively, we all breathed in as the car negotiated a narrow road, running between tall, whitewashed buildings, to finally reach Hostel Las

Terrazas, our haven for the next few days. This would be the perfect retreat to work on the book. We were situated in a small village called Bubión, nestled amongst other more sparsely populated mountain villages where you might, just occasionally, happen upon an isolated cottage. It was early November and I enjoyed the lush and fading greens, yellows, and reds with the dry rustle of leaves and twigs that had already expired. On our arrival, we were served fresh tomatoes, just picked from their vine and dressed modestly in herbs and olive oil, as we sat on the terrace appreciating the purity of both the taste of the tomatoes and the more rarefied air.

It was on this isolated terrace later in the day that Joyce asked José Luis if he would like a tarot card reading. I would very much describe José Luis as an earthly guide to Joyce and a friend to myself though the process of writing this book. By that I mean he has always very generously provided practical help to us both but has always been open about his skepticism and his need to qualify proceedings rationally. Although José Luis is fascinated by Joyce's mediumship, there is a part of him that also tries to explain away her gift. As such, I was not convinced that he would be entirely open to having this reading. In true José Luis fashion, however, he was receptive to the experience to see if he could learn from it. It transpired that José Luis was familiar with the different kinds of tarot cards and the different ways to conduct a reading. So, before the reading could begin, Joyce had to explain exactly how she would proceed; this was not one of the methods José Luis was familiar with and there was a brief moment of impasse. Joyce operates on instinct and has confidence in her method and so she thrust the tarot cards into José Luis' hands and, with her deep, authoritative voice, told him to shuffle the deck and stop when he was ready.

Joyce lay down two distinct sets of cards: one to detail his current situation and one to detail where José Luis would be going in the future. At the end of the first part of the reading, which outlined José Luis' current situation, while she and José Luis were discussing the cards, Joyce was visited again by the spirit of Angelina. Although it was not warm by this point of the early evening, the air was still and peaceful. A cool breeze suddenly made its way across the terrace, chilling us all. Joyce believes it was at this point that the spirit of Angelina connected with her again.

Just before the breeze signalled the arrival of the spirit of Angelina, José Luis had been challenging Joyce to identify the name of the film this line came from: "I am in the dark here!" I had heard them play this game several times. Usually, the context of their discussions would prompt José Luis to make a connection to a film they had watched together. They both established that the film was *Scent of a Woman*. In this film a blind man, literally in the dark, through helping a much younger character, is eventually saved from his own emotional and spiritual darkness. José Luis was not explicit about it, but knowing the film myself, I sensed that he was identifying himself with the blind man, played by Al Pacino in the film. Indeed, the tarot card reading so far had suggested that José Luis himself had been living through some dark times. The cards seemed to have triggered the connection to the movie in José Luis' mind. It was at this point of the discussion and moments after the spirit of Angelina returned to Joyce, that a most remarkably powerful thing happened. José Luis began to cry out, "Can't you see, I'm in the dark here!" At first I thought he was performing the line from the film again. But he became consumed by emotion and cried out again in greater desperation, "I'm in the dark here!" He began to sob, in obvious anguish. Joyce came from her side of the table and held José Luis in her arms, soothing him. Joyce quietly explained that this declaration, so sudden and powerful, combined with such intense emotion, was a cry from his soul. Once the overwhelming realization had registered, José Luis confided that he no longer wanted to be in the dark. The cards had made him confront his behavior patterns: his internal battles; feeling that his life was finished; his wallowing in past difficulties. For the past eight years, he had existed unhappily. Now it was time for him to take a bite of life and to enjoy the fruits of his long working life.

When the emotions stirred by the first part of the reading had settled, the second part, concerning his future, showed José Luis that it is his destiny to live in the sun and to be happy. Of course, whether or not he would choose to follow his destined path would remain to be seen since

Joyce has explained to me that the cards are never a guarantee of your future. This is because we all have free will. The cards may suggest a pathway that Spirit can see as a potential opportunity for you, but only if you seize chances that come your way. So, if the cards suggest a handsome guy is going to come in your life, but you decline the offer of a date from a handsome guy … you get my drift.

The spirit of Angelina continued to help Joyce with the rest of the reading by giving her insights into José Luis' state of mind. She told Joyce that she feels she lost connection with him when he was just three years' old. I was asked to leave the reading at this point since the spirit of Angelina wanted to share more personal information with José Luis about why he had felt so abandoned by her. The spirit of José Luis' mother confided in him, through Joyce, the reasons why she felt this connection had been lost and told him things he needed to understand about the context of his parents' marriage and his childhood that would help him feel less abandoned by her.

The experience of working with Spirit is very emotionally draining for Joyce; in this case not only did she have to face the anguish of her close friend José Luis, but also, even more powerfully, the distress of the spirit of Angelina. It was a particularly exhausting reading. Joyce, slumped forwards with her head on her arms, was overcome with tears that lasted for several minutes and she resisted our attempts to defuse them. Eventually Joyce sat up and hunched her shoulders, giving a small wry smile. She told us that the spirit of her father had just come to her and told her that while José Luis had now come out of his dark cave, she had now retreated into hers, just like the miniature figures passing each other on a Swiss cottage clock. It seemed poignant to me that the spirit of one of their parents had each come through to try and alleviate the sadness in their respective son and daughter.

Before we went to bed that night, Joyce asked the proprietor of the hotel, Francisco, if he had a problem with his shoulder. He replied that no, he didn't. Joyce shrugged her shoulders and we all bid each other goodnight. The following morning, Francisco rushed up to tell us that although he didn't have a pain in his shoulder, he certainly did now have a painful back! After our breakfast Joyce proceeded to give him the Reiki healing she had recognized he would need the night before. This involved laying her hands on Francisco's shoulders and back. He was amazed by the intense heat of the experience and asked if the heat was from Joyce's hands. Joyce placed her hands on his face so that he could feel how cool they were. The heat, Joyce explained, comes from the pure energy sent by the universe for the healing. In addition to being able to channel the energy of Spirit, Joyce has a healing gift and is able to harness energy from the universe for the purpose of healing. She then resumed the healing process with Francisco who was shaking his head and declaring, "Incredible." Again at the end of the healing, he grabbed Joyce by the hand and, again, to his bewilderment, could only feel coolness there. Joyce told him he should soon feel some relief.

Replete with our breakfast, the three of us decided to take a walk to the neighboring village, Capileira. This was a picturesque walk, allowing us to marvel at the majestic scenery and savor the fall hues that surrounded us. Many people take comfort from the beauty of nature and for Joyce, in particular, it is a means for her to restore some equilibrium following the emotional upset that follows an intense reading. It is for this reason that she enjoys taking photographs so that she can engage with and revisit the restorative images for when needs to remind herself of the beauty in this world. To take the time to really look at the colors of leaves, or the structure of a desiccated plant, allows us to live in the moment and to still our minds from the worry of our day-to-day issues. Joyce believes that when you are living simply and in touch with your senses, this is when you are more likely to be open to Spirit.

For as long as we could feel the warmth of the sun on our faces, we sat in the tiny square in the village, first on a bench as we watched two small boys playing in the water fountain, and then at the table of a tapas restaurant, sharing the plates of food placed before us. At this time of year, the temperature drops quickly in the mountains and so as soon as the sun began its retreat, we made our way back to our hostel in Bubión, retracing our steps in the now chilling air. At a sharp bend in the road, where a canopy of still lush green leaves gave it the feel of an enchanted tunnel, we noticed two female figures approaching us.

It became apparent that one of the ladies was Mari-Angeles, the wife of the proprietor of our hostel. As soon as she saw Joyce, she enthused that Francisco's back problem was now healed and that he had been in the orchard picking apples the whole afternoon. Evidently, Francisco was still completely overwhelmed by the power and effectiveness of Joyce's healing intervention. Very quickly, Joyce turned her attention to the lady standing next to Mari-Angeles and it was obvious that Joyce had made an instant connection with her. She started to talk to the lady, in English, telling her that she knew she had had a difficult life and that she was a very giving soul. Joyce hugged the lady who then spoke back to her in Spanish. José Luis translated the Spanish response for Joyce and explained that the lady, a friend of Mari-Angeles, is named Ascension.

Joyce made a very intimate connection to her and continued to hug her and to place her hands on her face, telling her that she felt like a sister to her. José Luis was concerned that Joyce's closeness may have been intimidating for this complete stranger, but Ascension reassured him that her son was a healer and she was familiar with such empathetic responses. Joyce was so overcome by the intensity of the connection between them that she spontaneously removed her ring from her finger and gave it to Ascension to wear. I know that this was one of Joyce's particularly favorite rings: a large yellow topaz mounted with tiny diamonds. Joyce explained to me that the energy of this gemstone is loving and positive so it was a perfect ring to be exchanged with a spiritual sister, surrounded by the wonder of nature.

Ever the pragmatist, José Luis later shared his concern that Joyce was going to have no jewelry left unless she devized another way to symbolize her connection to people. However, Joyce firmly believes that we should freely let go of possessions; having possession of a ring does not bring happiness in itself, but the giving of the ring and the memory of it does. The exchange with Mari-Angeles and Ascension consumed the remainder of the warmth of the afternoon sun and so we hurriedly continued our return journey to Bubión before we became too cold. The warmth of the real fire in the reception area was welcome indeed upon our arrival at the hostel.

As we reflected on the events of the day later that evening, we were joined by Mari-Angeles who had now herself returned from her walk. A subtle shift in Joyce's body movements, her eyes closing more frequently, ever so briefly, and her breathing becoming more labored, indicated to me that she was in communication with Spirit. Joyce announced to us all that Mari-Angeles is connected to angels. Joyce explained that in Spirit there is a hierarchy of spirit guides and an angel looks after Mari-Angeles. Joyce defines an angel as a being of light that is separate from other spirits. This suggests to Joyce that Mari-Angeles' spirit is one that is far advanced on the pathway to enlightenment.

As Joyce was connected to the spirit guides of Mari-Angeles, she was then joined by the spirit of Mari-Angeles' grandmother who came through to Joyce asking for her to advise her to take the wires out of her bras since she was at risk of developing a cyst in one of her breasts.

Joyce receives messages from Spirit at a very intense pace. Sometimes messages come so quickly that she barely has time to repeat them before a new one comes. Joyce very rarely can remember the details of a reading after the event, mainly because she doesn't have time to absorb them. In the case of her giving readings in Spain, this is made more complex by the fact that Joyce doesn't speak Spanish fluently. Somehow, the messages from Spirit always comes in English to Joyce. However, conveying these messages to her Spanish clients can be challenging.

Ordinarily, Joyce works with her translator, Pia, and they have developed a way of navigating this intense process. But it was José Luis who had to act as translator on our trip to Bubión: in one ear he had Joyce conveying many messages in English; in his other ear, he had Mari-Angeles qualifying or elaborating on the messages in Spanish. The dizzying effect and complexity of this activity could be witnessed on José Luis' increasingly exasperated face.

Joyce had told Mari-Angeles that she would have no further trouble with the knee that had been subject to several operations. Once we were alone again in the communal lounge, José Luis expressed his concern that this was a very bold statement to make: how could she be so sure? What if she had given Mari-Angeles false hope?

As an experienced entrepreneur, José Luis would naturally be concerned about a transaction being open to a challenge. I began to discern what I believed to be the heart of the conflict that José Luis felt concerning Joyce's mediumship. On one level, he was open to the messages Joyce would bring to him from Spirit: they made sense and captured an essential truth about him. I had seen that for myself during his most recent reading. And yet, this was a sphere that could not be regulated and relied purely on concepts like trust and faith. To a pragmatist like José Luis that seemed potentially dangerous. However, Joyce does not operate in the sphere of business, contracts, and liabilities. She had said what she sincerely believes and, in terms of connecting with Spirit, it is this belief and openness to believe which Joyce says is essential. By now, both Joyce and José Luis were exhausted and there was a tangible tension between them. José Luis just wanted Joyce to switch off from Spirit and relax and have fun. Joyce, however, was emotional and the events since my arrival had taken their toll on her so she retired to her room to rest.

This trip had been a much-anticipated break for Joyce; we had started it in high spirits which continued to rise as we wound our way up the mountain-side that first day. But the presence of Spirit is not something from which Joyce can so easily have respite. On my first night in Mojácar, and our first night in Bubión, the spirit of Angelina had emotionally drained "little Joyce"; on our second night, Joyce was again in her bedroom by early evening, leaving José Luis exasperated by Joyce's sensitivity while I contemplated the emotional cost to Joyce of her psychic gift.

When I later asked Joyce about why she always allows "big Joyce" to dominate the time and life experience of "little Joyce," she told me that "little Joyce" always feels constrained. "It's like wearing shoes which are too small so it hurts." Joyce has a strategy to help with the draining effects of her mediumship: "I try to never miss light, the chance to see a flower, to absorb everything that is beautiful." She is motivated by her desire to impart messages to help people, but she knows that this has a physical and emotional impact on her mind and body.

Our time on the mountain was spent and it was time to return to Mojácar. The descent of the mountain was undertaken in silence and it seemed that the intense emotional episodes of the previous forty-eight hours had cost us all some energy and our mood was considerably lower. I had found it draining to act as a buffer between Joyce and José Luis' fraught interactions and this is a role that would come to be reprised with them over the forthcoming months as I continued to work on the book.

Some hours later, the sight of the sea in Mojácar began to rejuvenate us all. In contrast to the perfect stillness we had left behind, the Mediterranean Sea was now more energetic with waves which bounced excitedly. We decided to share lunch together on the sea front and it was there that a lady tapped Joyce on the shoulder and then hugged her, thanking her for her previous insights. Joyce recalled that the lady's name was Concepcion and, coincidentally, she concluded the trio of meetings with ladies possessing religious names within the last three days.

A week later, back in the UK, I started to reflect on my own personal development. I was beginning to understand what Joyce was talking about in terms of being in the now and how appreciating the beauty of nature was a good way to do that. It is when you are in this peaceful state that you are able to listen to your sixth sense and become more open to Spirit. My last visit to Spain had been peaceful yet challenging too; it seemed to me that unresolved issues would continue to eat away at you unless you tackled them head on … or let go of them somehow. I sensed in myself a reluctance to let go of many things in my life. I was still substitute teaching between my stints in Spain, so I had not yet really walked away from my old life even though I knew I was unfulfilled and jaded by this. Spain was giving me insights into an alternative lifestyle, yet I still kept returning to the UK and things that were familiar. I sensed I still wasn't being brave enough.

4

Police Inquiry

Every trial endured and weathered in the right spirit makes a soul nobler and stronger than it was before.

W.B. Yeats

I started to resist seeing myself as a teacher since the target-driven culture of the education system had lost sight of the value of the softer skills and more holistic view of learning with which I so strongly identified. Instead of teaching, I decided to focus more of my time and efforts with research on the book while I was in England. I remembered that Joyce had followed up on a case with the police the last time she was there and had mentioned that she still had the contact details of one of the investigating officers. It would be good to get his take on things. I asked Joyce for his email address and she let him know who I was and that I would be in touch. He wanted to talk to me on the phone before he agreed to meet me. I could tell he was suspicious of me in the initial phone call ... and I was suspicious of him, wary of meeting a strange man and wondering what his motives may be in agreeing to see me. Nevertheless, I arranged to meet David at a motorway services station – the height of sophistication —on a bleak, wintery afternoon.

Joyce had already confided in me that it was while she was working as a professional psychic at her then local hotel that she had faced the greatest scrutiny of her career when the police became involved with a family she was helping. She was approached by a young woman who was distraught that a member of her family had gone missing. She was hoping to gain some insight of his whereabouts. But as soon as the woman sat in front of her, Joyce knew that the man was dead since he came to her in Spirit. This was a difficult situation for Joyce to handle. First of all, Joyce revealed just enough details about the man to allow Joyce to confirm his identity. She then proceeded to reveal more information that was so accurate the woman accepted that her relation must indeed have passed away. The family then contacted the police to let them know that they believed their loved one was dead.

The next day, Joyce had received a phone call from a colleague of David's at the police station wanting to speak to her about her reading with the woman. It was arranged that the police would visit her at her own home that afternoon. Joyce asked the officers to bring some of the dead man's personal possessions with them as this may help her to connect to his spirit and provide more information of the whereabouts of his body. More than a little concerned about what she may have become involved in, Joyce dressed herself smartly to give a good impression and nervously awaited their arrival. The police officers duly arrived and Joyce invited them in.

If Joyce was nervous about the visit, I discovered, when I met David at the grimy motorway services later on that January afternoon, that the police officers had approached this interview in a rather more dismissive and reluctant mood. I guess it's unsurprising that David, a police detective, was tall and imposing. He stooped to greet me, acknowledged that I was going to be recording the interview, then proceeded to present the details of his interactions with Joyce as if he were testifying in court. He was well-prepared and, unlike my interviews with Joyce, the note-taking process was clear and methodical.

Occasionally, I was diverted by the emblem of a small dolphin stitched on David's top. Joyce had once told me that I would soon find my dolphin—a romantic partner to sail the seas with. Michael was still procrastinating about whether we could make a go of things and I wondered if this was a sign that I should be looking elsewhere. I wasn't feeling any chemistry though so dismissed the thought. David explained that the family of the missing man had put so much pressure on the Senior Investigating Officer to listen to Joyce that two officers had been dispatched to see her just as a means of appeasing the distraught family. The police were treating this case as a "no body murder": this was a serious crime and they needed hard evidence to help them solve the case. Joyce's involvement was perceived as a nuisance and a distraction, likely to provide nothing more than a little material for office banter.

It was only at the last minute that David had become involved in the interview that day. One of his colleagues had called in sick that morning. David now found himself partnering the other officer, John, to question the psychic lady who they thought could help them with their enquiries.

David had joined the police after a military career and had spent the last decade working on serious crimes, including murders and police corruption cases. This is a man who is very experienced in dealing with people and who has undertaken advanced interview training. His job for many years has been to discover the truth of a situation and he does this by listening and evaluating: he believes it is not helpful to draw subjective conclusions about people and their actions as this may impede an investigation. David likens the truth to a piece of granite: it will hold despite the presence of superficial debris that initially may be obscuring its discovery.

On the afternoon of the interview with Joyce, the officers were dressed formally in suits and ties: as well as presenting a professional front, this also helped to neutralize their private identity. It was John who took the lead when exchanging pleasantries with Joyce and introducing his colleague, David, by his first name only. Very much taking a back-up role, David's police identification card remained in his pocket, and he spent most of his time observing.

David shared with me that the first thing he noticed was just how striking Joyce's appearance was: her heavily made-up eyes and long painted nails combined with her thick, blonde hair created a glamorous effect. She was bubbly and vivacious and joked with them, "Tea or coffee? … I guess I should know the answer to that!" David immediately warmed to her and considered her to be self-effacing. As is routine in cases of this nature, the police had already collected a number of personal items from the family and these were brought out at this point.

Once the drinks were made, the three of them positioned themselves in Joyce's lounge. John sat on one sofa with Joyce on an adjacent sofa. Completing the triangle, David sat himself on the footstool a comfortable distance away so that he could make notes and observe Joyce's body language. John led the way, with a flurry of questions. Joyce quickly told them they needed to let her flow before they could proceed. Some moments later Joyce had lots of information coming through from Spirit: she conveyed to the officers that the man had been murdered in a most gruesome way. The police already suspected this, but were hopeful that Joyce may help them to locate the body.

After about five or ten minutes of Joyce imparting information from Spirit, she suddenly spun her head to the right and asked, "Is your tummy okay?" David, somewhat bemused, replied that it was. A barely perceptible raised eyebrow was exchanged between the two men. Joyce continued receiving messages from Spirt. Again, she stopped abruptly and turned to him, "No, of course your tummy's fine, the problem was with your bowel ....You've had fives inches of your bowel removed." Barely concealing his amazement, he corrected Joyce, "No, I've had fifteen inches of my bowel removed."

"Ah, I thought they were showing me 1 to 5 inches, but they were showing me 15! But you're okay now." David confirmed that he had had bowel cancer seven years ago.

The exchanged expression between the two men shifted from one of skepticism to one of admiration and the entire mood and dynamic of the interview changed from that moment.

Once the investigation questions were completed, Joyce, who was still channelling Spirit, began to convey more personal information about the two men. She turned to John and said, "You're a bit of a bugger, you've been up to mischief with the ladies." John was indeed renowned at the police station for his extra-marital dalliances. And she informed David, "You need to get out of that marriage." No longer wearing his wedding ring, he had already accepted that his marriage was effectively over and just the previous week had consulted with a solicitor to begin divorce proceedings.

And so the officers' return journey to base was an interesting one. Neither of them had expected Joyce to know so much about their personal circumstances. Could she be playing us, they wondered? In the case of John, it was possible that Joyce may have heard local gossip about his extra-marital affairs. But it was not so easy to dismiss her knowledge of David's personal circumstances. He was only there in the first place because his colleague had called in sick and so Joyce could have had no idea he was coming. Yet it wasn't just Joyce's intimate knowledge of the men's personal life that was so disquieting, it was more so that they had to decide how to present the outcome of their interview with Joyce at the next briefing meeting.

Just because John and David were now more inclined to believe that Joyce did have some special ability didn't mean that the rest of the major incident team were going to suddenly welcome the input from Joyce: this was an environment where black humor and insensitivity were commonplace. It wasn't that the men wanted to persuade their fellow officers to become more in touch with their spirituality *per se*. Rather, they knew that if they presented the information concerning just the case to the team that it would be quickly dismissed. If they were to reveal the personal aspects of their encounter with Joyce, they realized that this would be the best way to validate Joyce's information—though it would leave them vulnerable to some personal jibes. So convinced were the men of Joyce's integrity, they both quickly decided that they needed to share the details of the entire meeting to the team. Yes, they were mocked by their fellow officers, but they had conveyed the truth of their experience.

The police agreed to work with Joyce in trying to locate a body. Joyce could see images of structures in the location where the body had been buried and, together with some police officers, visited numerous possible sites. In certain areas the energy was very strong and Joyce had the taste of copper in her mouth. Although the police deal in empirical evidence, Joyce recalls one of the officers looked uncomfortable and said that he could feel tension on the back of his neck. Joyce thinks this was probably the presence of Spirit. To allay his nervousness, she told him to say, "If that's Spirit, please go away." He instantly relaxed: Joyce is very adept at reading and defusing fear. Despite the strong energy on that particular day, however, a body wasn't found.

It was David and another colleague who returned to see Joyce to ask her to sign the statement she had made. He remembers that despite the persistent jeers of some of his colleagues, there was one officer who was particularly keen to go with him so that she could meet Joyce. David was reluctant for Mary to go with him; she was a spiteful person who always caused trouble with her colleagues at work. He was suspicious of her motives for wanting to go with him and felt she may present Joyce with a negative view of the police. He tells me that maybe he wanted to protect Joyce since he felt Mary would be a lose cannon and may make Joyce feel intimidated. However, he was overruled by his commanding officer and, in line with protocol, Mary went with him.

On this gray, depressing day David stood at the window in Joyce's home as she sat at the table looking over the wording of the statement. She glanced over at him and told him his aura was looking radiant against the gray sky. Joyce studied the aura more closely and asked him if he felt particularly energized. He paused for a moment and responded that yes, it was a good day. Joyce reiterated, "Yes, you have a very beautiful aura." From the other side of the room, Mary interrupted and asked, "What's my aura like?" Without looking up from the statement she had continued to read, Joyce replied, "You haven't got one, my dear." She had never met Mary before, but she had read her perfectly. David needn't have worried about protecting Joyce—she was more than capable of putting Mary in her place. Just in case you're wondering, we do all have an aura. The color and size of this will change according to the nature of the person and their emotional state. As a general rule, the more open and spiritual you are as a person, the larger and more vibrant the color of your aura.

David visited Joyce some months later to give her a debrief on the still unsolved murder. He had to concede that a lot of the information Joyce had provided had not been followed up, mainly due to limited resources. Also, because they hadn't been able to corroborate Joyce's information with anyone else's, the police did not want to be seen relying solely on the word of a psychic. And yet, away from the public and professional domain of the police station, many of the officers working the case went privately to see Joyce for readings—so impressed were they by her psychic talent.

And the outcome of the case? The information Joyce provided to the police had come from the spirit of the murdered person and she is in no doubt about how he died. However, the snapshot visions she received regarding the murder were never detailed enough to pinpoint the precise location of the body. Although desperate to help the family and the police, Joyce could only convey the information she received. Frustratingly, it was not enough. However, the spirit of the dead man conveyed to Joyce that he was grateful the police had got involved at all since he knew he had been such a source of trouble to them in the past. Above all, he was appreciative that the police were treating this as a murder case since it was very important to him that his children did not think he had abandoned them. His murderers have still not been caught and his family have not been able to bury his body. But Joyce knows that the messages she conveyed from Spirit helped this family to get on with their lives since learning that their missing loved one had not chosen to leave them.

The interview complete, David walked me to my car and stooped again, this time to kiss me goodbye, which took me by surprise. He said he would like to see and discuss the draft piece when it was ready and we arranged to have lunch together a few days later. During this lunch, I realized that he was interested in me romantically. My response? Embarrassingly, I started to cry into my dessert. His attentions made the grief I felt at the loss of other relationships surface very quickly. The poor man. He was very concerned and I had to explain that the tears were my problem not his. I was taking steps forward in my life, exploring the underlying reasons for my anxiety and low self-esteem with my therapist, Simone, but I clearly wasn't quite ready to meet my dolphin.

5

Spring Clean

The Spring comes in with all her hues and smells,
In freshness breathing over hills and dells.

John Clare

By February I had loosened the constricting shackle of my career, working just occasionally as a substitute teacher so that I felt I had the space to recover myself from the exhaustion of years spent working excessively which had left me little opportunity to meet the needs of my body and soul. It wasn't long before I turned my attention to another aspect of my life that was restricting me: the family home. I had always had an uneasy alliance with the house. I had lived there for over twenty years and raised my children there; but this was the house that had exposed the deceit in my marriage, that I had driven myself into the ground to pay for, and that reminded me of the most vulnerable times in my life. I knew I had to make another important decision and my gut told me I needed to go to Canada again. I had visited my friends there almost twelve months previously when I was struggling to recover from the burnout that resulted in my doctor signing me off from work. The distance away from my usual environment had helped me to get a sense of perspective and to begin to formulate my next steps which included resigning my full-time teaching post. I knew I needed that distance again.

During this second visit to Canada, connections with Joyce seemed to develop further. Visiting Halifax, Nova Scotia, I was excited to be able to explore the area with my camera and later uploaded my photos to Facebook. One of the shots was of a pavement slab: Cherry Street and Vernon Street were etched in the concrete. Spotting her name, Joyce responded to my posting instantly. "It's written in stone . . . . A sign indeed!" she joked. Joyce was referring to her absolute belief that Spirit had brought me to her to write her story and felt that my accidental discovery of her name was a sign from the universe that everything was going to plan and that she was part of the reason I had come to Canada. And the "Vernon" connection didn't end there. My Canadian friend, who works in publishing, revealed that his middle name is Vernon and, when he later mentioned the book to a local publisher, he was introduced to the editor whose name was … Vernon! The universe seemed to be nudging us to carry on with the project of writing the book.

While I was there, I felt an inner peace and clarity of thought; I was really able to listen to myself. My house was an empty nest and I didn't see why I couldn't fly off from it too. I resolved to put the house on the market as soon as I returned home. Yes, my head kept saying, "Are you sure?" as it felt the panic of losing control. But my heart stood firm and I received an offer for the full asking price before the FOR SALE sign was even put in the garden. A sign indeed that the universe felt I was doing the right thing.

Upon my return to the UK, and having agreed the sale of the house, I decided it was time to commit to the book more fully. I resolved to return to Spain in the spring and to stay there until the book research was finished. And so one warm, sunny afternoon, I found myself standing on a sidewalk in Almeria with Joyce who had gone to the city to "smudge" an office for a lady who felt it was filled with bad energy. I could still smell the burning sage from the smudge stick as we waited for Pia to collect the car. It was a tranquil Sunday afternoon and the streets were empty as people were probably sharing some family time. At first we did not pay much attention to the coach-style pram that was being pushed towards us by a very elegant young Spaniard. As the pram moved past us, there was instant connection between the upright baby boy, about eighteen months old, and Joyce. They became united beneath the beaming sun as they exchanged smiles and kisses, the baby having relinquished his soother instantly, the better to blow a series of joyful kisses at Joyce with his tiny extended hand until she became lost from his sight. Joyce was radiant from this spontaneous encounter.

Joyce told me that it is by reminding ourselves of our younger, freer spirit that we can shake off the shackles of adult responsibility and become more in tune with our spiritual selves. The child within Joyce has a very special connection with children and is like a magnetic pull to them. One of the reasons she has such a strong connection with children is that she still sees the world with a child's eye: she is open, honest, and trusting. Babies and children see, and are drawn to, the light and love in Joyce. She explained to me that our souls always seek love and will rejoice, and long to remain, in its discovery. Children instinctively feel this and search for a potential source of love. Unfortunately, this is what makes them vulnerable in our society where this may be exploited.

Joyce had a busy schedule that day. As well as the office cleansing, there were four readings booked at her friend's place. Leo's house is situated at the edge of a new sprawling development at the very top of a mountain. It is one of just three houses in the cul-de-sac. Leo, short for Leonora, welcomed us enthusiastically and had prepared a lunch for us before the afternoon's readings. Joyce, Leo, and Pia began to reminisce about one of the first times Joyce had done a reading there. They all remembered fondly the visit by the man with the bag of potatoes. Sensing my interest, they were eager to share the whole story with me.

Joyce had just finished a reading for another client and had begun to walk her client out of the house, when Leo came to her in a very agitated state to tell her that there was a man at her gate asking to speak to the English medium. Leo was confused that a stranger had found his way to her remote house, situated high on a hillside and was even more disconcerted by the fact that he knew that an English medium was there since these were private readings that she had arranged. One of Joyce's key spiritual guides appeared next to her and Joyce knew instantly she would be helped to manage this situation. Joyce told Leo not to panic since the tall, locked electric gates didn't need to be opened until they were reassured the man was genuine.

There were two stages to opening the gate. First, Leo needed to activate a buzzer from inside the house and then a key could be used to unlock the gate. So Leo returned to the house, leaving Joyce and her translator, Pia, on the driveway where she could see the man behind the closed gates. Even though Joyce had advised her to keep the gates locked, and that was what Leo intended to do, she found herself pressing the buzzer inside the house. A buzzing sound emanated from the gates. Leo went out to reassure everyone that it still needed the key to be opened. Instantly, however, the gates began to open by themselves . . . .

A middle-aged man who had a round figure with short, bandy legs and was dressed informally in shorts and t-shirt walked through the gates. He told Pia, who spoke Spanish and who he assumed was the medium, that he was in turmoil. Pia pointed him in the direction of Joyce who instinctively gave the man a long hug. He confided, "I don't know who I am or why I'm here." He told Joyce that his car had driven him to the gates and he had no conscious recollection of how he had arrived there. I had just arrived there myself, and, trust me, this is not a house that you would just happen upon. Joyce was told by her spirit guide that he was from Egypt and had travelled through Morocco; he was a man who lived simply and grows vegetables for a living. Being a clairsentient, Joyce is able to feel sensations communicated by Spirit and she felt, against the skin of her chest, a pendant which she saw was a Sufi pendant indicating that this was a very spiritual man. Joyce could see that the lost man usually sits on a rock by the sea to meditate.

All of this information was conveyed to the man and Joyce emphasized that he needed to be wearing his pendant so that he could feel more at peace spiritually. His hand went to his chest and from beneath his t-shirt he pulled out a Sufi pendant. Joyce explained that his spiritual guides, sensing his stress and turmoil when he had become lost, had sent him to see her. Joyce did not know what had caused his memory lapse, but realized that her role was to enable the man to return to his home. Reassured, he opened his wallet to give Joyce some money, but it was empty. Desperate to provide some recompense, he offerred to give part of the pendant, a gold coin, to her. Joyce refused this generous gesture; it was payment enough that the spiritual guides of this man had sent him to her, confident that she would be able to help him on his way. Besides, Joyce knew that the pendant was a significant religious icon for the man and would not dream of taking this from him. In addition, Joyce felt very strongly that the lost man needed to have some turquoise and she mentioned this to Leo who she knew collected precious stones. The day before she had been sorting through her jewelry collection and had come across a turquoise scarab. For some reason Leo had left this piece to one side, separate from the rest of the collection. Instantly, she knew for whom the turquoise scarab was meant.

This story is a commendation of Joyce's psychic ability since the spiritual guides of the lost man had faith that she would be able to help him. She feels very proud of this. The man insisted on offering some form of recompense and a few minutes later returned from his van with a bag of potatoes for Joyce. On his journey to see Joyce, he hadn't known why his van was full of potatoes. Now that she had helped him to remember, he understood that he made his living growing and selling potatoes in his home village.

After lunch when the anecdotes were finished, the first of Joyce's readings arrived. Gabriela had been to visit Joyce on several occasions. She reminded Joyce that in one of the previous readings her grandfather had come through and told her to buy a lottery ticket as she was going to have a big win. Gabriela now told Joyce that there had been no such win. However, she went on to say that she had bought the number 673 as she thought this was her grandfather's number. When she failed to win, she decided to check with her mother what number he used to buy and was told 473 and 573 … and both of these numbers had won the week she bought her ticket!

Gabriela's brother, Pablo, had died from stomach cancer when he was still a young man. Since then, Gabriela had been visiting Joyce as a means for her to look out for and protect her family: would her children be okay? What about the health of her mother—was there anything to look out for? Since the death of Pablo, Gabriela was also concerned for the welfare of her nephews, Pablo's sons.

The spirit of her brother came through at this reading which I was given permission to witness. I positioned myself some distance from Joyce, Pia, and Gabriela, as I didn't want to invade the intimate space between them. They were on chairs, huddled in a small circle, while I sat on some cushions at the edge of the room. Joyce said that the spirit of Pablo was quite intrigued by me and he had come to sit near me. This did unsettle me somewhat, especially since a moment before I had felt a cool breeze brush my cheek. I had looked over to the window to see if it was open, yet I discovered it to be fastened shut.

Pablo's spirit thanked his sister for looking after his boys and reminisced with her, through Joyce, about the fact that he was better than Gabriela at evading their parents' wrath when they had been young so that they had always thought him to be an angel. The spirit of their grandmother came through too, joking that she was thankful her eyesight went at the same time as her beauty so she remained blissfully ignorant of the effects of aging. Grandma reminded Gabriela to light a candle for her brother, explaining that just as Spirit, the term for collective spirits, puts light into earthly situations, a lit candle puts light into theirs. It shows Spirit that they are still loved and thought about which means a lot to them. It is a compassionate idea to light a candle and send the light into the darkness.

Pablo's spirit would like to be Gabriela's guide as she herself is about to start and give readings to people. He tells her that he has recovered from the sadness he felt at dying so young, but that when she becomes sad about his death this makes him sad again, too. Joyce advises her to remember passed loved ones when enjoying positive experiences, even invite them along to join in, for example, at family celebrations. Think of them as still being there rather than being dead. She uses the analogy of being in a car. We don't feel any different whether we are in or out of our car. If the car is likened to being our body, the spirit doesn't feel any different being in or out of the body.

Gabriela was told that when she feels the sensation that she needs to clear her throat, which has happened since her brother died, that is the spirit of her brother trying to connect with her. As the reading ends, he tells his sister that she is beautiful and that he loves her, telling her to relax and enjoy her life. Finally, Pablo tells his sister that they are soul mates and that the first thing she will feel when she passes are his arms around her. This was a wonderful reading to witness: Gabriela was comfortable with Joyce and with connecting to Spirit and this felt a bit like a family gathering, with light-hearted jokes and quips interspersed with advice and genuine concern for one another.

The following reading that day, however, did not flow quite so easily. A middle-aged woman arrived with a searching, fearful, face. She had seen Joyce a year ago and was keen to let her know that after the last session she had felt very relieved to know that her loved ones were living on in Spirit although she still was feeling her grief very acutely, finding it difficult to accept that they were physically gone and so still waiting for her loved one to walk through the door. She desperately wanted to know if there was any way Joyce could give her some concrete evidence that her lost loved ones were with her?

Immediately, Joyce told the woman that there was a female spirit standing right behind her who looked just like her. Joyce asked if she had recently lost her mother to which the woman replied no. Several family spirits came through quickly to Joyce and there was some discussion about who had come through first and who was who. Joyce established that it was the woman's mother now stood behind the chair. Very quickly, a male spirit was pushing to come through and so Joyce asked if the lady had lost her father. She responded that, yes, she had, many years ago. The spirit of her father came through and he wanted to talk to her about the loss of her mother. This was confusing to Joyce since the lady had said her mother was still alive. At this point, however, the lady confirmed that her mother had indeed died more recently.

Joyce became aware that the lady who had come for the reading was so anxious that she wasn't really listening to what Joyce was saying and was putting obstacles in the way of connecting with Spirit. It was for this reason that she had answered Joyce's question incorrectly at the start of the session. Joyce reassured the lady that her mother's spirit was standing behind her, touching her face, talking to her – that she often came to talk with her daughter. Joyce gently instructed the lady that she needs to be relaxed and open to be able to connect with Spirit and sense that they are there. The more you consciously try to connect the harder it will be. The lady's mother had difficulty swallowing at the end of her life and Joyce told the woman that when she feels this sensation it will be her mother's spirit trying to connect with her.

Another spirit came through, a male, who was desperate to kiss the lady on the cheek. Joyce said it was her brother and that she has a very strong connection with him and that he's been with her all her life. The lady was not aware that she had a brother, but says that her parents wouldn't have talked about a lost child in their day. Joyce explained to me later that the spirit of the brother would not necessarily still be an infant since spirits live more than one life, continually evolving, and are able to choose how to present themselves to Joyce. The father's spirit went to his daughter and kissed her on the head and Joyce, who is clairsentient, was able to feel his heart swell up with such a wave of love for his daughter. Joyce told her that when he pops into her head that is when he is with her.

With the connection to family established, the mother's spirit told her daughter she is with her everyday and suggested that she buy a spare pair of glasses as she would soon lose a lens out of hers. The spirit of her father interjected and suggested she reinforce the glasses with glue so that she doesn't have to waste her money buying another pair. Her father then told her that she hasn't been singing enough. The client told Joyce, "I don't sing." The spirit insisted, "You used to sing like a sparrow when you were a little girl." At this point the lady gently nodded her head and agreed, "Ah yes, when I was a child." Joyce told her he tries to put songs in her head for her to sing.

The spirit was sad that he had placed more value on earning money than spending time with his family. He had listened to Joyce and I talking about the man with a bag of potatoes earlier; he told Joyce that people would be happier if they lived more simply rather than spending their time making extra money that won't really bring them happiness. He became emotional and said what a gift his daughter was in his life and that he was happy that she wasn't feeling the weight of missing him and his wife. Joyce saw him give his daughter a geranium and advised her to have plants around her and to invest in a little more happiness in her life, for example, by playing music in the car. Although there wasn't a physical geranium for her to take, the daughter nodded in appreciation of the gesture Joyce was describing. He ended by saying, "Don't forget to get a cake for your birthday – we'll be there to blow out your candles!"

So there was another lady, surrounded by the warmth of Spirit, her grandmother, father, mother, and brother all eager to come and give her advice and to reassure her. And yet there was an uneasiness in the atmosphere and a sense of unfinished business. Joyce asked the lady, "Is there anybody else you wanted to speak to who hasn't come through?" Immediately, the energy slumped and there came a heaviness in the room which was oppressive. The lady told Joyce she desperately wanted to speak to her daughter. Joyce saw that the daughter had died very suddenly. Joyce explained that the daughter's spirit had been resting. This means that she had not been visiting her loved ones very frequently as the spirit needed time to come to terms with what had happened to her. Her death had been traumatic with two doctors debating the best way forward as her condition took a sharp decline.

When spirits can see that you are distraught, they don't always like to come through as they aren't sure this is what you want. In this case, Joyce could sense distress on both sides. Just like the mother sat for the reading from Joyce, the spirit of the daughter sat with her arms folded, in a state of agitation. Joyce explained that this spirit was still not eager to talk and seemed reluctant to get too close to her mother, even though she had come through. She was guarded, trying to contain the anger she felt at her sudden death. However, this spirit wanted to ease the pain of her mother. The spirit of the daughter asked Joyce to tell her mother that she was sorry for leaving her. Joyce explained to the mother that when she cries, often these are the tears of her daughter's spirit. In the mid-afternoon when the lady sits and has a little cry that is when her daughter is with her. The spirit of the daughter apologized for making her mother tired and she thanked her for being such a good mother to her.

Joyce could see a little ring being held out by the daughter's spirit and asked the lady if this meant anything to her. It turned out the lady was wearing a ring that belonged to her daughter. The spirit of the daughter explained she didn't feel it was fair that she went when she did although she admitted that she gave up fighting. The spirit didn't want to leave the reading on this low note so she told her mother how she loves the spirit of the maternal grandfather she never met. They go for long walks and talk about everything. Joyce told the lady her daughter is beautiful and that she tries to connect with her every day by pressing on her neck or giving her the smell of oranges. The spirit told her mother, through Joyce, that mortal life is not the end. In life we have worries, anguish, and shackles; however, the afterlife is paradise compared to this. She asked her mother to buy herself freesias, telling her she would love them, especially the yellow ones.

Joyce says it is the love and personality that continues on in Spirit so it is important to think positive thoughts while on earth since love is a lasting memory. Spirit urge us to be outside in this beautiful world and take the time to stop and look at the flowers. This family of spirits had been trying to show this lady rainbows and butterflies. The spirit of her father advised her to notice the little flowers in the roadside. He told his daughter that passed loved ones haven't disappeared from your heart so they haven't disappeared from your life. His final message to his daughter was, "Go with a big smile and a lighter heart and give us time to talk to you." The loss of her daughter had left the lady's heart shrivelled like dried fruit. It is the beauty of life that plumps it back up again. Although it is difficult to have an open heart and look outwards when you are hurting so much, this really is the way for you to start to heal yourself, safe in the knowledge your passed loved ones are no longer in pain and are with you in Spirit.

It was sobering to watch. I recognized that the experience of observing Joyce give these readings was indeed helping me to heal. If these people who were so burdened by grief could find a way to look outwards, then surely I could too. So much time had I spent working! Missing opportunities to walk in the sunshine or just relax with my children. What had all those years on the relentless hamster wheel been for? I began to sense I was emerging from a very dark tunnel.

When we got back to Mojácar, Joyce received a message from her niece to say that Joyce's sister's health had declined suddenly. Liz had been ill with cancer for several years and this left Joyce to decide when would be the best time for her to go back and see her. The doctor had given Liz a maximum of a month to live. When Joyce asked Spirit if she would see her sister again, they had responded that she would, just one more visit. This confirmed to Joyce that her sister would not defy the doctors' prognosis this time and also reassured her that she would get to England in time.

Joyce trusted that she would speak to Liz again in Spirit, but knew it was time to face the fact that Liz wouldn't physically be in her life for very much longer. Joyce had been dreaming of her mum and dad and so she knew that they were getting ready to come for her sister. Just like the rest of us, Joyce has to deal with the fact that our friends and family are mortal. Being a medium doesn't make this any less painful for her.

Joyce felt at peace with the knowledge Liz was going to die, but felt it was unfair for the end to come so quickly, "When a family member is old and wrinkly it is easier to accept." Joyce believes, however, that you go when it's your time. You may imagine that because Joyce leads such a spiritual life this makes facing death easier; however, Joyce uses the analogy of a parachute to explain that although you know it is safe to let go and that there is something and someone to catch you, it still requires a leap of faith. Joyce decided to go as soon as possible to spend some time with her sister and support the family. Death by cancer is not kind, and not just for the person dying, but for the entire family. Joyce knew she needed to be there so she could see her mum and dad come for Liz in Spirit and to comfort Liz's family.

6

Root, Shoot, Twig, Tree: Cutting Life, Isn't It?

The sea is your mirror; you contemplate your soul
In the infinite rolling of its surface.

Charles Baudelaire

Over the years, Joyce has done readings for many people who have lost loved ones to suicide. She feels the responsibility to be accurate even more strongly in these cases since she appreciates just how much heartache there is. When Joyce has someone with her who has been hurt by the loss of their loved one, it is so important to her that she eases their pain by convincing them of her connection to Spirit.

Joyce has found that the information is always given to her by Spirit in enough detail to convince the loved one of this connection. The mood is then quickly changed with gentle humor from the person in spirit. The personality always comes through strongly and making someone laugh at this moment is such a healing thing for both the spirit and their loved one who is reminded of how they were before they became ill.

Before Joyce left for England to attend to her sister, she invited Robert , an Irishman now based in Mojácar, to come and talk to me about his son, Kian, who had committed suicide. Robert had heard that I was writing Joyce's book and he was keen to talk to me to raise awareness of death by suicide and to discuss its impact on those left behind. Kian had been independent and successful, but his life was greatly affected when he suffered terrible injuries in a horse-riding accident. Although the injuries were significantly life-altering, Robert is still now trying to understand fully how this then resulted in his son committing suicide.

The first thing that Robert shared with me was the way that his perception of, and reference to, time has been altered by his son's suicide. In Robert's mind, time exists in two halves: the time before the loss of "my boy" and the time after he died. While the rest of us think in layers of the past, a single now, and a multitude of imagined futures, for Robert those nuances have gone: his life has been limited in terms of the way he perceives and categorizes it. *Before. After.* A starkly reductive perception. Robert lets go of his sadness, from time to time, by sharing this with a closed bereavement group on Facebook, where other people who have suffered a similar loss provide support to other members of, what Robert calls, this "horrible club."

When asked how he met Joyce, Robert explained that one day, after Kian's death, he was sitting in a bar listening to a guy he knew sharing his experience of a very weird encounter with a medium called Joyce. The friend suggested that he might benefit from meeting Joyce. Robert is Irish, "Catholic by birth, failure by practice." His Catholic upbringing instilled in him that suicide is the worst form of death, it being considered a sin, and as such it had a lot of guilt attached to it, an uneasy feeling that his son's actions may have offended God. Robert can accept that we are all going to die, that it's part of the natural order. The suicide of his son left him not only with grief, but with a paternal guilt: his son hadn't shared his troubles with him so Robert felt he must have failed to support him or be a good enough father.

Seeing Robert's suffering, his friend made the appointment with Joyce on his behalf. Robert knows that he would have put it off indefinitely, reluctant to meet Joyce out of fear and skepticism. Even at our interview, he tells me he went to see Joyce only to satisfy his friend. Robert admits that he was a little curious and as our discussion develops, reveals that post-Kian's death, he looks for enhanced meaning in all possible places, for example, lingering on the interpretation of a dream that may have been blinked away pre-Kian's death. I began to detect a reason for Robert's initial reticence to see Joyce. "Do I want it to be successful because I need it?" He was concerned that he might try to make things fit just so that he could be reassured that there is indeed an afterlife and, if he just bides his time, he will be reunited with Kian.

Robert did want the reading with Joyce to be successful and he would have been disappointed if he had left the reading without any sign of the afterlife or Kian. I asked how could he be sure, then, that the reading wasn't just wish-fulfillment? Robert understood my question. His default mode is skeptical and anything that Joyce mentioned that was in anyway generic, such as commenting that Kian was a handsome boy, he ticked off in his mind and rejected as "bits of shit." Yet he conceded that there were two aspects of the reading that were just too specific and accurate for him to dismiss. Indeed, these two facets were so profound that they frightened him: Joyce could not possibly have known these things.

First of all, the spirit of Kian, through Joyce, used the following words: "You're doing it again and I asked you not to, don't over-think it." Kian was slightly cross and was reprimanding his father. Robert has told me that the opening line of Kian's suicide note included these words: "You're going to be sad, but don't over-think it." The repetition of those words astounded Robert and have had a powerful impact on him as he realized Joyce could not possibly have known about the contents of this letter. Secondly, he was amazed, not so much by other things that were said, rather by the way Joyce conveyed the spirit of his son to him, through gesture and turn of phrase.

Robert felt like Joyce wasn't there and that he was having direct conversation and banter with his son.

Before this reading, Robert had become consumed by the need to be with Kian. The guilt was making him feel he needed to atone for his perceived failure as a father and look after him better in the next life. Robert confessed to me that he had become depressed and suicidal, caught up in the "warped logic" of suicidal thoughts. Joyce was able to confirm that Kian was okay and that Robert didn't need to join him. She helped Robert to see that his own suicide would be completely unnecessary.

Reassured, Robert took medication to help him to overcome his depression and now is challenging the stigma attached to mental illness. Robert agreed to talk to me so that this book could help to raise further awareness of some of the issues that may lead to suicide. He can't understand why society is afraid of medication to help our mental illness, yet not so to help us with physical ailments. If our heart rate is uneven, we can use a pacemaker to regulate it. Likewise, if our brain develops a chemical imbalance, which may result in depression, there is medication than can help rectify this. Robert asks, "Where does this stigma come from?" He believes that gender stereotypes have contributed to the fact that two thirds of suicides are of men. Countries with a "macho" culture tend to have higher male suicide rates than others. Women talk and confide in each other whereas men don't. Why? Sometimes suicide is about the only control you have left and that's a very sad reflection of our world.

The interview with Robert made me realize that the impact of suicide is always distressing, sorrowful, and brutal. After Robert had left, I spent some time reflecting with Joyce who believes that if you don't work through the difficulties in your life, you will have to have face them in the next life. In addition, you will still be alive in Spirit and will see the repercussions of the suicide. Those left behind will have to navigate feelings of guilt, anger, and bitterness. Suicide fails to resolve anything: it perpetuates chaos and misery, leaving peace and tranquillity elusive. Sadly, suicides are often committed in a state of desperate confusion or when someone is suffering with mental health issues. The tragedy is that the person committing suicide cannot see that there is always another way.

Despite the warmth of the sun and the glitter of the sea, the terrace was very subdued as Joyce shared her experiences of helping relatives come to terms with the loss of their loved ones through suicide. The mood became even more melancholy as Joyce began to pack her case to return to the UK to see her dying sister.

We decided that I would stay in Mojácar and work on the book. As if in sympathy with Joyce's sad situation, the sun disappeared the day after she left Spain and the rains came … and came. I had plenty of material to write up so I burrowed myself into Joyce's small apartment and pecked away at my laptop. José Luis would brave the torrents of rain to bring me stew or soup to warm and feed me. From the wall unit, Joyce's treasured photograph of a Rinpoche would gaze out at me while the photograph of the side profile of her mother seemed to contemplate the far-reaching familial branches.

It was Sam who rescued me when I was on the brink of becoming stir-crazy. We went for a coffee and ended up downing several bottles of beer and glasses of wine. It seemed we had both been starved for a bit of company while the heavens had opened in the past week. Joyce had initially stayed with Sam when she first came to Spain. Always a tricky matter to share an apartment with somebody, Sam says that it's an altogether different matter to live with a medium. He confided in me that she would sometimes have tearful and restless nights. In the mornings, bed-sheets would be a tangled mess with smudges of mascara on pillow-slips and her glamorous blondness would be coils and clumps of frizz. I knew just what he meant: I too had witnessed the tears and the chaos when "little Joyce" had been worn out by "big Joyce."

As Sam and I both know from our time spent with Joyce, you may not be wanting a reading although this doesn't mean you won't still get messages from Spirit, through Joyce, from time to time while you're in her company. When she is with her friends, sometimes the distinction between "little Joyce" and "big Joyce" can become blurred. On one occasion, Sam confides, a deceased friend of his came through to Joyce. She and Sam had been sharing a drink or two and this let Joyce's guard down so in came the spirit of Pete who, in life, used to recount all of Sam's past license plates to him as a party trick. She began to relay the plate numbers exactly as Pete would have done—and they were all spot on. Sam remembers this was the first time he felt he had actual evidence that Joyce was an authentic medium.

It was a few weeks later, in late May, that Joyce lost her sister. Liz died, surrounded by her family, and Joyce saw the spirits of both her mum and dad appear to come and get her. Joyce would be staying for the funeral and to help the family to come to terms with Liz's death so I went back to England to work with her there. I stayed with my parents as they lived fairly close to Joyce's family and we were able to see each other a few times each week.

A week or so after the funeral service, as we chatted, Joyce became a little dejected and said, "Who's there for me?" Small Joyce was tired and just wanted somebody to look after her. She wasn't sad about the death, rather, she felt it was like an amputation of her energy. "Anybody who has lost a loved one or a much-loved pet will understand the absence of energy when you walk into a room when they have gone. For so many years, Liz had been a focal point for me. After her death, I feel energetically unbalanced." Joyce knew she just needed some time to reacclimatize. She knows Liz is alright, still there, but on a different plane. "You just can't WhatsApp them."

In the middle of our conversation the spirit of Liz came through and held her hand. Sitting there with my laptop, I suddenly felt a surge of warmth in my body. Joyce explained, "Liz is connecting to you. Hey, she likes the book! Oh, and she wants to know if you can get me to swear less." I joked that was unlikely. It seemed that just when Joyce felt in need of support, her sister was there to give it to her.

The following day, Joyce received messages from two of Liz's friends saying that they had dreamt about her sister the night before. When Joyce asked what she was wearing, they both described her in the same way that Joyce had seen her. When I did some research about this, I discovered there are examples of these kind of visitation dreams that have been well documented by many other people. It was clear to Joyce that her sister's spirit had been doing the rounds that night to say her goodbyes.

Although we were back in England, the sun had followed us there. There really is something very idyllic about a glorious summer's day in England. The sun seems gentler somehow and time becomes suspended as people submit to the hazy, lazy warmth and the intoxicating aroma of grass and flowers. Days such as these are perhaps treasured and indelibly marked in the banks of memory because they are so rare. Yet that summer, days like these became endless. Joyce and I would sit in her friend Sarah's garden, the place where we had first met less than a year earlier. How far we had come together in that short time, how much I had learned of another world, another way to live.

From time to time, Sarah, also a medium and Reiki healer, would come and join us as we worked and one day she agreed to tell me not only how she came to be connected to Joyce, but also her personally tragic and harrowing story that made both she and Joyce question whether they could continue to be mediums.

Many years ago, after Joyce divorced her husband and moved out of the Cheshire village, she was quite surprised to be reunited with a connection from her past when an attractive young blonde girl turned up for a reading and Joyce learned that her name was Sarah ______. Joyce recognized the family name and told the young woman that she knew a family of this name in the village. It turned out that Sarah had married a local lad, Andy, from a farming family in Cheshire and that Joyce had watched him grow up.

Joyce lets me know she was very proud when Sarah later started to do readings for people, "I have worked hard for my reputation and will proudly recommend my friend for readings without hesitation. She feels like a daughter to me." Joyce was included in their family life and, when she used to go and visit, Andy would be adamant that she couldn't leave until he had seen her. "He used to joke with Sarah that he had always thought I was fit for an old 'un!"

In the early stages of her psychic development, Sarah would still go to see Joyce for readings since these would be more specific than the information Sarah could glean as a novice. Sarah would keep notes of all of her readings with Joyce and share these with her husband. They were so accurate that Andy, who had initially been skeptical, decided to make a visit for himself. His paternal granddad came through, as was typical for the readings Joyce had done previously for Sarah. Andy came to rely on Joyce's readings which proved to be so accurate with respect to details of both his personal and professional life. It became a pattern that whenever there was a problem in their lives, Andy would send Sarah to see Joyce and everything that came through would be written down on sheets of paper.

In bed at night, Andy and Sarah would go through the notes to see what had happened in their lives subsequently that correlated with the reading. In one reading Joyce channelled Andy's grandfather who told them that they would get the old family farm back. This came to pass. In fact, everything that the spirit of Granddad relayed over the course of these readings came true. "When Andy's extended family bought back their former farm, they sent Andy to manage it. I would go and call for a cuppa or stay to have some supper," Joyce chipped in as we sat in Sarah's garden discussing these events.

Andy had always been desperate to run his own farm, but soon after they had bought back the family farm, a reading with Joyce had warned that they would only have three years of happiness there. But Sarah and Andy's marriage was very secure and together they felt they could face anything. Even a less optimistic reading from Joyce.

During one visit to the farm, a few months later, with the fire roaring to warm them against the fall chill, Joyce gave them another reading. This time the spirit of Granddad came through, but with a different demeanour: he was reserved and tearful. "They are going to pull the rug out from Andy in March and there isn't anything we can do about it." Joyce saw Andy literally having a rug pulled out from under him. The farm had been experiencing some financial difficulty and it was assumed that the bank was going to foreclose.

Joyce was told by Spirit that the main family member, presumed to be Andy's father, would die. Joyce saw a tornado ripping the farm in half and was told that this death would precipitate the downfall of the business. She saw a funeral cortege with two hearses leaving Andy's parents' farm, a separate location from the farm Andy was managing. Joyce suddenly felt a bang on her head as though someone had hit her with a cricket bat: "I assumed that Andy's dad, who had actually had a stroke sometime previously, may be about to die. I could also see a ring that would need to be re-sized and I was told that there would be sadness at the maypole dancing." Understandably, they were all very subdued after the reading.

Six months later, in March, Joyce was sitting in her apartment when her friend and landlady walked in and said, "Andy's dead."

How could she not have seen this coming? With later reflection, Sarah remembers that she had become incredibly insecure about her relationship with Andy in the weeks leading up to his death. Repeatedly, she would ask him, "You're not going to leave me, are you?" Andy felt that their marriage was secure and grew irritated with her growing anxiety. With hindsight, Sarah knows that she was sensing his death, knowing deep inside that he was indeed going to leave her.

Sarah explained to me that she had returned home on the day Andy died and had become suspicious that his lunch was still untouched on the counter where she had left it hours earlier. None of his laborers knew where he was and so a frantic search of the farm was made. His body was eventually recovered from the bottom of the slurry pit. Sarah remembers that one of the reasons it had taken them so long to find Andy's body was that she had not been able to sense his spirit. Joyce has described to me how it is usual for Spirit to collect, very quickly, the spirit of those who experience a traumatic death so that this spirit is spared from witnessing the horrific impact of their death on their loved ones left behind. That frantic search was heart-breaking and Sarah remembers bartering with the world of Spirit "upstairs" as she had tried to resuscitate him once he had been pulled from the slurry pit.

It is Joyce's belief that angry spirits are not allowed to encroach on the space of people here uninvited. She has explained that they simply wouldn't be allowed to turn up and dominate anybody's personal space and cause upset.

Joyce was in her own apartment when, unusually, she sensed the presence of a very restless and angry spirit.

Already berating herself for having been unable to foresee Andy's death, Joyce was not prepared for his spirit to come through so quickly, on the evening of the day he had died.

When Andy started to convey his anger to Joyce and she realized who it was, she collapsed to her knees in grief. Joyce had not yet been to see Sarah, yet knew that she would have to face her and let her know that Andy's spirit had come through to her.

Joyce turned up at Sarah's the following night. Her face red with raw emotion, she came across to Joyce, "I don't know what you've come for. I don't want to speak to you." Joyce tried to stay calm as Sarah continued to scold her, "Why didn't you know it was Andy that would die? He trusted you!"

Joyce breathed deeply to steady herself, "You're right and don't you think I would have walked barefoot over hot coals to have avoided this? But Andy's spirit has come and said he's got things he needs to say. Do you want to hear or do you want me to go?"

Sarah wanted to hear.

The spirit of Andy, calmer by now, came through again to Joyce to let Sarah know how the accident had happened. He was able to reassure her that he hadn't drowned in the slurry. He had slipped, striking his head on the side of the slurry tank. The blow to his head had killed him before his body had subsequently fallen in the slurry. He was upset that a careless slip had cost him his life, but he also recognized that it was better for the children that he had gone before Sarah; he and they would not have thrived if she had died first. Sarah came out of the room with Joyce feeling calmer than she had been.

Following Andy's death, Joyce was at first unwilling to engage with Spirit. How could she trust herself to read cards for others if she had got it so wrong for her own nearest and dearest? It took her and Sarah a considerable amount of time to realize that the tarot cards she regularly used during the readings did accurately predict the future. But, at the time, the cards had presented the events of the future ambiguously. Both Joyce and Sarah would soon see that the signs for the future were accurate after all.

Andy had died in March and in May, when it would have been his birthday, which coincided with the early May Bank Holiday weekend, the villagers were in tears as they danced around the maypole, just as had been predicted in Joyce's reading. Sarah had retrieved Andy's wedding ring from his body and later took this to be re-sized so she could wear it. She ruefully acknowledged that this had been another detail from Joyce's reading that had come true, although it hadn't made any sense to her at the time.

As predicted, the family business was ripped apart by Andy's death. Sarah is convinced that it was the horrific nature of his death that ultimately provided for her and the children's future. The bank staff responsible for the foreclosure of the farm had sleepless nights and felt the plight of this innocent family. A deal was struck with Sarah that allowed her to purchase another property, subject to a reasonable mortgage, by the bank.

The image that had most convinced Joyce that it was Andy's dad who was going to die was the fact that she could see the funeral hearses beginning their journey from the parents' farm, not from Sarah and Andy's farm. When the funeral was arranged it was Andy's parents who had insisted that the funeral hearses leave from their property. Both Joyce and Sarah are able to take some comfort from that: the cards didn't lie.

In her darkest hours, Sarah lost her ability to connect to Spirit. In time this recovered, as did her trust in the universe. She knows that Andy is her soulmate. This meant that they had both made a pact, before their spirits were re-incarnated, that this was how things were going to be for them in this life. Despite the tragic loss of Andy, Sarah knows that she would do it all again, to be able to have the precious, though short, time she had with her special husband.

For Joyce too, this experience was one of the greatest tests of her faith and trust in Spirit. Little Joyce feels grief just like the rest of us. But she also knows how to listen to her emotions effectively. There is no point directing feelings of anger, guilt, and betrayal at Spirit or allowing these feelings to consume your life. With time for reflection, Joyce could see that the card reading was accurate.

It is the interpretation of the cards that is subjective and Joyce is especially mindful of this and feels the weight of responsibility that comes with her psychic ability.

7

On the Road Again

The only business of the head in the world is to bow a ceaseless obeisance to the heart.

W.B. Yeats

Having lived in the company of Joyce, at first in Spain, but latterly in the UK, I began to be more conscious of the ways that Spirit is always giving me little signs and nudges. In May, I had a particularly vivid dream during one of my last nights sleeping in my house in England, in which I saw a herd of wild horses. They were predominantly black, but with a few white horses on the edge of the herd. Constantly moving in circles, some were lifting their forelegs, gyrating in the air. Watching them, I was suddenly filled with strength and energy. Initially, I had felt afraid of their power, but then I looked into the eye of the lead mare and knew that these horses had been sent to reassure me rather than to threaten me. When I was properly awake, I felt resolved, energized, and excited about moving forward with my life and that there was nothing to be afraid of.

While in the UK to sign the paperwork for my house sale, I managed to meet Joyce's eldest son, Chris. With his mother's large eyes, Chris conveys a nonchalant attitude to his mother's psychic ability. When I asked him about the impact of his mum being a psychic, he merely shrugged his shoulders and smiled as he joked that, thankfully, he'd already left home before she had realized the full extent of her powers! Modest and charming, Chris was more interested in how I had come to meet his mother and how the writing was progressing. It was Joyce who informed me that he is developing his own psychic talents. Although he had not yet been to visit his mum in Mojácar, he had been able to describe to her over the phone when she first moved into the apartment at José Luis's, that if she went out of the gate, turned left, and walked up the hill, the road would bend to the right and open up to countryside. He told her she would find a very flat rock that she would be able to sit on. Joyce confirmed to me that she had subsequently made the walk and sure enough had come across the flat rock that was large enough for her to sit on.

I had hoped to catch up also with Joyce's younger son, Tom, for an interview while in the UK, but his shift work had made this difficult so we managed to video chat instead one evening when I was back with Joyce in Spain a couple of weeks later. I had decided to return to Joyce and push on with the research for the book while I waited for the sale of my house to complete. Tom described himself as having felt somewhat skeptical in the early days of his mum's life as a medium and he would always be asking questions of Joyce: "How do you know *this* isn't *this*?" While his intelligent and enquiring mind had a healthy respect for what his mum did, he always felt he needed concrete proof before he would be able to be fully convinced of her veracity.

It was as a young adult that Tom got the proof he was looking for. He had a very good friend called Steven who had had a heart transplant. Sadly, Steven subsequently died from a heart attack at the age of twenty-one. Tom had been working with him on the day he died. Steven had felt unwell and gone home from work early. Unfortunately, because of the heart transplant, he had suffered nerve damage and so had not been able to feel the typical symptoms that would alert you to the fact you may be having a heart attack.

Not long after his passing, Joyce told Tom that Steven's spirit had come through to her and that he wanted to have a word with him. It would turn out that Steven's visit provided Tom with the proof that he needed that our spirit doesn't die with our body. He described working with Tom at the hotel where there was a long rectangular room that was often used to host wedding receptions. Steven explained to Joyce that quite often, when he and Tom would work a shift together, they would be caught in the room listening to endless rounds of speeches. To break the monotony, they would chop up fruit and throw it at the wall, out of sight of the guests, to see if they could make it stick. Tom confirmed with me that this was true, but that he had not shared this information with anybody else – it was just a joke between Steven and himself. This was the proof he needed that his mum must truly be channelling Spirit and that he was in the presence of his friend, Steven.

From this point on Tom began to engage more with his mum's activities. Joyce had always encouraged Tom to read people – even before they have opened their mouths— prompting him to reflect on his response to a person he meets for the first time and to consider whether he is detecting a positive or negative energy. Tom reminisces that she urged him to never be afraid of being silly and to do something that would impress your eight-year-old self. Tom says of his mum, "She is amazingly strong, yet incredibly soft."

Tom, an extremely intelligent and sensitive person like his mum, now uses tarot cards himself, but he still can't explain how it works. He does know that you have to practice, a bit like learning a musical instrument, a little every day. His advice is not to question it, but rather to "just do it and go at it honestly." His final counsel is that if you were to wear earmuffs and a blindfold, cutting out what you're used to relying on, you would be able to listen better to Spirit. I began to appreciate that Joyce's connection to Spirit isn't something that can be explained through logic. There isn't a magic formula to help you to understand how to do it. It's about openness and trust.

The completion of the sale of my house took me back to the UK again. I was beginning to sense that I had more than enough research to start to pull the book together. But with the reality of selling my home now upon me, I began to feel some doubts. I had hoped that by this time I would have a clearer idea of my next steps, but they still seemed to be eluding me. Finishing the book project was a certainty, but where was I going to live?

Stoically, I pushed fears and doubts to one side as I handed over the keys; it was time for a younger family to write their stories there. It had been another hot June day and, as I drove away from the town that had been my base for over forty-five years, I became aware of the most spectacular sunset on the horizon. My eyes were drawn upwards to three birds flying in a 'V' formation as if escorting me towards my future. A feeling of warmth and elation surged through me. I didn't know where my next home would be, but I knew that I had made the right decision and that I was going to be alright. The future would be beautifully bright, just like the sunset.

Before I worked with Joyce, I had not been aware that people look out for signs from Spirit in this way. Once I was conscious of this, I too started to notice more signs. A couple of weeks after the sale of my house, I was walking through an unfamiliar town, looking to see whether it could be a potential place for me to buy a property. As I walked, a sense of dislocation began to grow. It was a beautiful summer's day and the town was lovely, but I felt no sense of belonging.

Just as I began to feel a bit overcome by this, a thought popped into my mind, "You need a reason." It then made perfect sense to me: location itself wasn't a sufficient purpose for me. I needed a person or a project to lead me to the place I needed to be. I was approaching a busker on my side of the street and I began to listen to his lyrics. "I'm on the road again." This refrain was repeated a few times, then, just as I was walking right in front of him, he sang an extra line, "Looking after my soul again." I beamed at the busker and a feeling of happiness and trust ran through me. It wasn't time for me to worry about buying a house or to think about where would I end up living. I still needed to leave my heart open to opportunities that may come my way.

Was this a sign from Spirit? I'm unable to say to you that it definitely was. What I can say, absolutely, is that by noticing my environment, I felt so much happier. It seemed remarkable that the busker was singing lyrics that meant something so personal to me at the very moment I passed him. Joyce is convinced that when you see order in disorder, a pattern amongst the chaos of life, this is usually Spirit trying to give you a sign.

I was packing my bag again, this time to go and visit an old school friend of mine to get his opinion on the content of the book so far. I was still in constant communication with Joyce and would notice, increasingly, that my phone battery would frequently show 69% charged. So persistent was this number 69 in my life that I decided to ask Joyce what it was all about. "Why don't you just ask them?" she messaged back. Well, because I don't talk to them the way you do, I muttered inwardly, but wondered what would happen if I tried to ask the question. I remembered Tom, Joyce's son, telling me not to try too hard, just to go with it. So I lay back on the bed and tried to get myself into a more relaxed state.

After some time just focusing on my breathing, I asked the question in my head, "Why do I keep seeing the number 69?" Quick as a flash of lightning, I saw a series of distinct images in my mind's eye: A Canadian flag, a desk laid out with writing materials situated next to a window that looked out on a cold and snowy landscape. It wasn't exactly the answer I'd been expecting. Rather, it was more like a dream where I felt I would have to interpret what it all meant.

The Canada part was straightforward to me. I had already arranged to go there again in July to help my friend, Una, make the road trip from Ontario to Nova Scotia where she was moving to be closer to her daughter and to have a fresh start having been widowed. Could it mean that I would stay longer than the anticipated couple of months I had envisaged? Would I still be writing the book there in the winter? I was perplexed, but beginning to realize that you don't get answers all at once from the universe. I remember Joyce telling the ladies at the development group that it's a good idea to keep a journal so that you can record information you receive to cross-reference later. It's too easy to dismiss a sign just because it doesn't make sense to you at the time.

The following morning, I woke up with a thought in my head: I had left Canada, the place of my birth, to return to the UK with my parents in 1969. So, it seemed that 69 might have something to do with Canada. I would have to wait and see.

But for now it was time for me to visit my friend in the North-East and show him how the book was shaping up. I gathered up my rucksack and set off for the bus station, a far less stressful way to travel than navigating airport security although I could have flown to Joyce in the time it took me to make my way north to Newcastle-upon-Tyne, and the vicinity of my family's old stomping ground, Middlesbrough. My grandparents had long since passed and it had been years since I'd regularly ventured up here.

I wondered if I would feel any sense of "home" here? But the gray, rainy motorway vista did little to inspire me.

I made my way to my friend Martin's place, an urban loft apartment in the heart of the city. We shared a couple of cocktails as I unpacked the details of the past nine months since I'd last seen him. It was then that I had first told him of my plans to work with Joyce. He couldn't wait for me to reveal the details of the book and the next morning we made a start looking at how to sequence the material. Frequently, I would lift up the laptop lid after a little break and find that it showed 69%. I told myself I was looking for the number now and to try not to obsess about it too much. That night, as I snuggled down to sleep on the sofa, I noticed that the battery charge was 58%. I smiled knowing that I could not possibly see 69% in the morning . . . .

When I woke, I folded the sheet and blanket to one side and got ready to resume work. I had left the document ready to pick up at the penultimate chapter of the book. I opened the laptop lid: 56%. Okay, good. Then I navigated to the open document. Instead of showing the start of the new chapter where I left off, I found myself in the middle of a chapter from much earlier in the book. It had skipped backwards. I huffed out loud as I tried to figure out where I was in the document. I looked to find the page number … page 69! What was going on here? Why was I being shown this number all the time? It came to me that I should read the contents of page 69 to see if this held any clues. It was the part where I was having my first lunch with Joyce and she had spotted my maple-leaf necklace and I went on to reveal to her that I was born in Guelph, Canada. So, the number 69 did seem to have some connection to Canada. Was Spirit endorsing, prompting even, my decision to return there?

With some semblance of a draft now ready, I left Martin and the North behind and returned to my parents' place, my temporary abode, to pack a larger case to take me to Canada, beginning to feel that maybe there was a sense of destiny at play here. I decided to let go of my worries about buying a house and finding some place to settle … I was going to go with the flow and see what would transpire.

Less than four days later, I was flying to Toronto with an utterly blank canvas. I had no plans other than to make the road trip with Una, finish the book, and see whether my friend, Neil, who has a professional background in publishing, could help me get it published. Hours later, as the plane began its decent, the air steward prompted us all to look out of the windows to both our left and our right since we were in the middle of three planes in the process of landing simultaneously. The air steward explained that this was a very rare occurrence. The thought and the image took me back to the night I had left the family home for the last time and saw the three birds flying into the sunset.

By midnight, I made my way wearily from the elevator towards my friend, Una's apartment.

"Oh my, I swear to G-o-d, you looked just like Heidi as you walked down the hallway," Una yelled as she peered more closely at me, maybe to determine exactly what it was in me that reminded her of her daughter.

She relayed the marvels of our similarities to cousin Myrna and her husband, Murray, over dinner the following evening.

"And, would you believe, the insurance brokers now need to see a 'letter of experience' before they will insure

Louise to drive my car!"

"Oh no! What about the road trip?" sympathized Myrna.

"W-e-l-l-l, I guess I'll have to do the driving and Louise will navigate."

Murray raised his brows in response to Una's declaration, "All one thousand miles, Una?"

"Y-e-s-s-s!"

Murray met my gaze.

"You're so brave!" consoled Myrna.

"I reckon Louise is the brave one," interjected Murray to his own amusement.

"Well, you know you are so adventurous to make this move, Una."

"It took me a while to come to my decision, but I'm settled to it, Myrna."

"Good for you and you both have a safe trip," hugged Myrna not wanting to let go of her cousin.

"Stay in touch," encouraged Una, "And if you're ever travelling east. . ."

* * *

As Una busied herself with final preparations for the big move, I had been in touch with Joyce to do some work on the book. During our chat she told me that attention needed to be paid to one of Una's toes, the big, right toe. I asked Una to stand in front of me so that I could see what may be amiss. Cautiously, I looked down at the foot. Oh my God, what was going on with that toe? "Dear Lord, Una, what happened to your toe?" She explained she had lost the nail circa 1985 when, as a teacher, she had gone out on a community walk with her special needs kids. One of the "big fellas" had run over her toe while pushing another student in a wheelchair. I reported this to Joyce, explaining that, having now seen the hideous toe that missed a nail, it was better it didn't have close attention!

On the Friday, the packers arrived early. Joyce had given me the heads up that the guy was really cute – and he was! He had a limp as he had broken his ankle and so was on light duties. But this didn't hold him back any. Once I realized the way he operated, I darted around the apartment scooping up the essentials Una and I would need for the road and stuffing these into an "out-of-bounds" cupboard.

The blue-tooth speaker blasted out tunes as they packed at a lick while Una scrambled to gather her undies and I stashed the kettle and tea-bags.

On Saturday, Una took me to an empty car lot so that I could get used to the feel of her car and the ways of using an automatic. The 'letters of insurance' had been sorted and I would also need some practice driving on the right-hand side of the road. I adjusted all my mirrors and felt like my eighteen-year-old self, having my first driving lessons. Una explained I just needed to press the button and move the gear shift into R for reverse or D for drive. How hard can that be? Very as it goes … at one point, we both had both our hands on the stick, tugging at it. The shift wouldn't shift. Exasperated, Una came round to the driver's side and asked me to get out so she could get in, "For G-o-o-d-d's sake! Wh-a-a-t-t am I not telling you?" I stood and watched as Una settled herself into the seat. Instantly, she had her eureka moment, "The brake! You need to keep your foot on the brake before you can move the shift." Once that was established things went swimmingly.

Eventually, we were ready to start our road trip. We made good progress on the first leg and were settled into our beds in the motel in Cornwall, still in the province of Ontario, for an early night. Leaving her old apartment that had been her home with her husband for many years was going to be hard and Una was feeling vulnerable, telling me she wished she could have a sign from her late husband, Peter. Una has always been a very spiritual person and she is open to the idea of Spirit giving us signs. She explained that he usually left her dimes to signal that he was with her. That morning, we stopped at a coffee shop for breakfast before starting the second leg of our journey. As Una returned to her seat, a guy called out, "Hey, lady, is this your dime?" On the spot where she had stood lay the dime, the sign she had wanted that her husband was still with her in spirit, supporting her choices.

We were quite excited at the start of day two, but little did we know what the province of Quebec would have in store for us. Una had written down the directions from Neil. Route 30 then Route 20 East. Stay south of the river. That was it? For the whole of Quebec? No sat.nav.? No road map? It all seemed rather broad-brush strokes to me. The only assistance we had was the atlas I'd insisted on buying. To be fair, we went great guns for a few hours. There was a moment of consternation when we saw a sign that said, "30 FIN" with no visible sign for "20 EST". But there was a coffee shop on hand with free Wifi and some very helpful French-speaking Canadians. In particular, a very sweet older man who wanted to explain that the roads to 20 EST were good even though they weren't highways. Additionally, and more philosophically, he reminded me that the road may seem long since it was unfamiliar, but not to worry—it was not so long as it would seem and we would soon reach 20 EST. With hindsight, that little sojourn really was the least of our worries that day.

We really did feel kings of the road when we found "20 EST". This road would take us into New Brunswick – surely we were on the home stretch for that day. Not quite. We still had the snarly tangle, as it appeared on the atlas, of Quebec City to deal with. Each "20 EST" sign was a triumph! Until Una decided to overtake a "slow turtle" truck. The pang of dismay was keen as I saw "20 EST" peel off to the right and we peeled off to the left. We were crossing a bridge, headed north ("NORD"). We needed to stay south of the river. This wasn't good.

We pulled over as soon as we saw a coffee shop and parked up to plan our next move. We were stood outside of the car getting some air and puzzling over the atlas. Fortunately, a knight in shining armor came to our rescue and said we could follow him in his car. Our poor ability in French-speaking was a barrier so he squeezed both hands to mimic a flashing signal and said he would let us know when to take the road left back over the bridge to the south of the river. Re-orientated and with the comfort of "20 EST" flitting past my passenger window, Una confided, "Well, I wouldn't be in a rush to kick him outta bed!"

On the third day, we made the final leg of the journey through New Brunswick and Nova Scotia. The closer we were to reaching our final destination, the more impatient we became for the long trip to be over.

"Louise, would you please just look for a sign to tell us how much farther it is."

"Sure." I was keen to know myself when I would be able to stretch my legs. In the distance I saw a large, green sign. I had my glasses on, but I needed for us to be closer to see what it said, "Halifax 69 kilometers, Una."

Oh my days.

8

Three Steps to Personal Freedom

Happiness is neither virtue nor pleasure, nor this thing nor that, but simply growth. We are happy when we are growing.

W.B. Yeats

And so I came to spend a few months in Canada redrafting the book and just enjoying being there. I had no firm plans, was living day to day, and learning to appreciate what it meant to live in the now. I had cut off all my old ties and was giving no thought to the future. I realized, vaguely, that I probably wouldn't be able to sofa-surf indefinitely and that, at some point, I would need to generate an income stream for myself. But even that didn't seem too urgent as Neil was really busy and needed extra editors to help him with the jobs that came his way. So while I tidied up the book, I did some freelance editing work that helped me to rent a room and feed myself. Did I miss my house or my stuff, most of which I'd given away? Not at all.

I had time to reflect and realized that I'd failed to listen to my own needs and wants for years, even decades. I hadn't been able to trust myself anymore because I'd lost sight of who I really am. You may wonder why would somebody who had been so organized and so accomplished choose to throw herself into such chaos? The answer, I now realize, is that it was precisely this chaos for which my creative spirit longed.

I remembered that when I was about twenty years old, I had a feeling that I needed to return to Canada. I didn't have a plan or a specific reason, it was just a feeling. Eventually, I ignored my feeling as a silly whim and settled instead for visits from time to time over the years. Yet here I now was, back in Canada. I wondered if this was something I had been meant to do a long time ago. When I asked Joyce about this, she explained that I am exactly where I should be at exactly the right time. Joyce firmly believes that we are evolving spirits, learning our life lessons as we go along. Whatever I was learning from being in Canada, it was not until this point in my life that I was ready to listen and be open to my inner voice. This, I now realize, isn't a silly voice. Rather, it is a truthful voice that your rational mind sometimes argues against, especially if this voice is suggesting something unconventional.

For too long, I had ignored the voice that whispered to me I was unhappy and needed to make some changes. I recognized that my soul had been weeping for a long time. The cracks had been showing in my façade until that day they had ruptured entirely, triggered by watching a film that made me realize that I had compromized on my dreams for too long. I would go to bed crying and wake up crying, for days and weeks. I stopped functioning. I couldn't work, I couldn't carry out domestic chores, my body didn't even tell me when to eat. It was around this time that I began to hear a knocking sound inside my head. It was so clear and loud I would ask my son if he could hear it too, but he never could. On other occasions, I would hear somebody say my name, yet I knew that I was in the house alone. I really did think I was beginning to lose my grip on reality.

The time had come for me to heal myself. I wasn't quite sure how I was going to do this. Then I met Joyce. I had confided in her some of the details of the stress and anxieties I had experienced the previous year. She has explained that the calling of my name could have been Spirit trying to get my attention and letting me know they were there for me; the sound of my name would have been inside my head, rather than an actual sound in the room. Likewise, the sound of the knocking that nobody else could hear would have been inside my head. Joyce thinks Spirit must have been getting quite exasperated with me by this point and they were trying to knock some sense into me!

My inner voice had been suppressed so many times, it just didn't bother speaking to me anymore. I know that having opened myself up to listen to what my emotions are telling me has given me a happier life. Joyce would argue that by also listening to the signs and guidance that Spirit provides, we can avoid some potential difficulties and feel more secure in the choices we make as we live our lives.

Living with a psychic has been an intoxicating experience. First there is the adrenalin rush from the pure fear of the unknown, then there is the warm embrace and you find yourself longing for just that bit more soothing, like a baby who knows the scent of comfort and instinctively clings to it. You become sucked into an alternate universe, a world where money and property have scant regard while trust, freedom, and happiness mean everything. Joyce has shown me that it is okay to walk away from unhappiness. She has also shown me that if you truly believe you deserve the best in life, you will receive the best in life from the universe. That's the trust part. And as with any relationship, it is the cornerstone.

If I have learned one thing after living with a psychic for a year, it is that courage is everything. And I'm not talking about the courage to face the world of Spirit, but to face the ghouls and demons that haunt your daily existence. With courage, you can live rather than exist, love rather than fear, and be your true self rather than the person others expect you to be.

Over time, we will change and evolve so what made us happy when we were ten is not going to be the same as what makes us happy when we are forty. As Yeats signalled, "We are happy when we are growing." So, after living with

Joyce for a year, what do I consider to be the three crucial steps to personal growth?

1. Listen to your emotions and walk away from unhappiness – you will find peace in this empowerment. Your needs are important. If you deny these, you deny your own existence and your self-esteem will become eroded;
2. Be brave – never let convention or fear of failure or of the unknown stand in your way. I gave up a salaried career, sold my home, and gave away most of my belongings. I have never felt freer or happier;
3. Live your life rather than exist. Relish the present and realize your true purpose. Treasure the small moments and feel gratitude for what you have. Stop waiting. If you feel your true purpose has become lost, remind yourself of what you enjoyed as a child: this could give you some important clues.

It is surely time that we all begin to reflect on the things in our lives which are compromising our happiness. We all need to take time to listen to the needs of our soul which will do its best to nudge us into making changes to improve our happiness.

9

Take It or Leave It

We all have a better guide in ourselves, if we would attend to it, than any other person can be.

Jane Austen, *Mansfield Park*

In many ways, Joyce is an ordinary person just like the rest of us. She has a mischievous quality and I came to see the way the edges of her mouth twitch in readiness to burst into bellowing laughter; it's very easy to find yourself giggling in Joyce's company. She would have been a great friend to share your school days with.

Yet there is also considerable depth to Joyce. She has lost loved ones. She's been unlucky in love, married and divorced, twice, and has been a single parent. She has been a victim of domestic abuse. At times, she has struggled with health issues. To many of us, Joyce's world is very extraordinary. She believes that we have experienced past lives. She believes that we all have spiritual guides who try to help us through our life's challenges. And she believes that we are spirits living a life in a human body and that our spirits never die, rather they evolve.

Naturally, Joyce would argue that these beliefs and her profession are not extraordinary to her. She feels it is her purpose to help to develop people's spirituality. For her, the medium's job is to help everyone. Joyce sees people who range from the cynical to the desperate. As such, giving readings is an exhausting process, drawing on her emotionally, psychologically, and intellectually. But she has boundless warmth and wit to help her.

Her convictions about spiritual matters come directly from her personal experience and from the remarkable gift she has to receive communication from Spirit. Joyce has no wish to confront those who may have an alternative view of this. She understands that some people rely solely on logic and empirical evidence and so may remain skeptical about her beliefs.

On many occasions, I have asked Joyce how she would want me to explain the reason that she is so staunch in her belief of the existence of Spirit. Each time she has given me the same answer, "It comes from my own experience. Just because I can't explain it, doesn't mean it isn't so." She qualifies this by emphatically telling me that she has seen angels as well as spirits although she recognizes that there is no way that she can prove it.

Joyce does not feel that it is her purpose to convince you. She does not wish to recruit disciples or cast stones at those who have different beliefs. Rather, through this and our subsequent books, she wants to share with you the benefit of her own spiritual and life experiences. People may come to a greater spiritual awareness at different times in their lives. Some, however, will never open the door. Joyce accepts this.

During one of my summer visits, Joyce had been having one of her own reflective days: the process of writing this book had reminded her of some of the ways she had been let down by others and of some of the painful situations from which she had learned. Spirit had been communicating with her intensely on this day and she had been accompanied by a particularly poetic spiritual guide well into the early hours of the morning. I heard the restless creaks from the sofa in the adjoining room. As I lay in my bed, too hot to sleep, the suspended wooden angel seemed to nod at me in agreement as I wondered whether I sensed Joyce channelling Spirit.

The following morning, I woke to read a very detailed posting from Joyce on Facebook so that others could learn from her own experiences. This was so powerful that I decided to shape the poetic prose into a poem to end this book.

* * *

Naked Truth

(*Inspired by Joyce's wise, poetic words and the guidance of Spirit.*)

There will come times in your life when you don't
crumble, or collapse, but just feel the need
to lean for a little while …

Treasure these moments of illumination,
seeing truth in all its unsavoury
glory laid bare …

Your imagined heroes will disappear
as an early mist in the sun, leaving you
on the beach …

Watching their sails recede into the horizon:
this is a true moment of awakening.
Grip it tight …

Beware letting it fall wasted in the
sand at your feet. Face this dawn: feel the
warmth of this new sun …

Dry the bitter tears of disappointment
on your cheeks. Leave the memories of bitter souls
at your feet …

Look only to the future, the promise
of this dawning where you can step forward
without disenchantment

With those who professed their love and support.
Step away from those discarded robes of
false promise and respect …

Stand naked if needs be. But know, in your
soul, you are real, free, not susceptible
to others' whims and fancies …

Lift your face to the sun …
and breathe.

Epilogue

A year after I first met Joyce, I had completed the first draft of my book. It had been like trying to tie down a cloud as I caught hold of the disparate parts. However, it still wasn't sitting quite right so I decided to go back to Spain for the winter and spend some more time with Joyce. I had purchased my tickets to the UK so I could see my daughter and son before then flying on to Spain. I was even thinking about renting an apartment there for a spell.

It was very early October and I had just two more weeks in Canada. One day, Joyce called me. "I'm seeing you in Canada in November."

"I can't see that," I replied, "I've already bought my tickets – I'll see you in a couple of weeks."

"I don't think so. You're going to meet someone. He's younger than you, very handsome. I can see him. He's

Canadian or American, I'm getting mixed signals, definitely North American."

"I hardly think I'm going to come back for somebody I haven't even met yet – it's already October."

"I'm just telling you what I'm seeing. I really don't think you're going to be with me."

The closer it came to the date of my departure, the more thoughts of leaving Halifax preoccupied me. I reasoned I could come back after the winter and that Spain would offer a cheaper way to live for a while. As if to taunt me, it had been an active week on the dating site, Bumble. But I was resolute that the Canadian bees would have to wait a little while.

I decided I would swipe right on men where I felt I could generate some good karma. So, the first match was with a guy who had a very sweet profile. I messaged him to let him know I liked his warm smile, explained I was going to Spain, and told him I was sure his profile would attract the right bee for him. No response, which was fair enough. A couple of days later, another match. I did the same thing, explaining I liked his use of humor and wishing him good luck in his search for his bee. This guy actually messaged back to thank me and said to enjoy Spain. (This guy understands karma and I suspect he will find his bee soon.)

I told myself it was time to stop. I'd had my karmic result and now it was time to shift my attention to returning to Europe. On Thursday, however, another "like" drew me to the Bumble page. And there he was.

I so wanted to connect to him. I feared he might dismiss me once he became aware of my unconventional context. Even so, I went for it: "Hi, I'm flying to Spain on Sunday to live there while I work on a writing project. I couldn't resist swiping right when I saw your profile. I wouldn't usually be so bold, but would you like to meet for coffee before I go?"

"Hi Louise. That's quite the intro! Sure, I'm up for meeting. Is the goal to make me fall fast and hard for you within a few days before leaving the country?" he joked.

By the following Wednesday, less than a week after I swiped right, we had both fallen hard and fast and I had cancelled my flights to Spain and booked my return flight to Canada. Oh and just to clarify, he is Canadian, but his father had been in the military and so he had spent a chunk of his childhood living in America when his father was stationed there.

* * *

Want to know more about Joyce?

Read about how Joyce came to realise she was a medium and the countless people she has helped to connect with their loved ones in our second book: *How to Live After Death*

"Joyce is a warm, loving, selfless soul."
Sharon

"Blimey! She described my present life as if she knew me … such a talented lady with a heart of gold who showed me, and shared with me, the true meaning of life."
Jane

Joyce is one of the most remarkable women I have ever met. Her readings have stayed with me because so many elements of them have come true. There are so many things that I would like to say to Joyce but I just don't know where to begin.
Josie

Extract from How to Live after Death

An uneasy silence greeted Joyce as she became aware of her surroundings. She was alone in the living room and found herself lying on the sofa. Her throat was incredibly sore and her eyes gradually came into focus and settled on the clock on the wall. It was 1:00 a.m. A surge of panic rushed through her now conscious mind: where was he? Was he still here? Her hand went to her tender throat as she recalled the violent outburst of her husband. *He tried to strangle me.* He must have run off, assuming that he had killed her. Joyce knew she and her baby son couldn't be there if he came back.

Frantically, she crammed a few carrier bags with baby clothes, food and toys, and a few personal items. The McClaren striped stroller was loaded with the make-do luggage and her small, sleeping son. This was in the time when not everybody had a landline telephone let alone a mobile. She had friends living nearby, but it was the middle of the night so she decided to walk the two and half miles to her mum's house. It was November and cold as she struggled to push the laden stroller through the quiet streets and lanes. Feeling completely alone in the world, Joyce looked up into the black night and said inwardly, "If there is a God, He is a bastard." As if in reply, an icy cold rain started to fall torrentially from the sky.

It took Joyce a couple of decades, and many more difficult experiences in her life, before she came to realize that she was not alone on that evening and that she was indeed being helped . . . .

Purchase your copy here:

www.joycevernon.com

~

Contact Louise & Joyce:

instagram.com/louise._piper

instagram.com/vernon.joyce

Printed in Great Britain
by Amazon

35176996R00106